WOMEN AND VIOLENCE

Library of Congress Cataloging-in-Publication Data

Levy, Barrie.
    Women and violence / by Barrie Levy.
        p. cm. -- (Seal studies)
    ISBN-13: 978-1-58005-244-3
    ISBN-10: 1-58005-244-4
    1. Women--Violence against. 2. Women--Crimes against. 3.
Women--Social conditions. I. Title.
    HV6250.4.W65L49 2008
    362.88--dc22
                                        2008019055

Cover design by Kate Basart, Union Pageworks
Cover illustration © Lauren Simkin Berke c/o rileyillustration.com
Interior design by Michael Walters
Printed in the United States of America by Maple-Vail
Distributed by Publishers Group West

WOMEN AND VIOLENCE

BARRIE LEVY

SEAL
Studies

*To Charlie, my dad . . . mentor, professor, promoter of justice and ethics,
and my grandchildren's playmate*

CONTENTS

PROLOGUE

I AM A DAUGHTER OF THE 1950S. I started my adult life in the civil rights, antiwar, and women's rights movements of the 1960s. The culture I grew up in had rigid taboos against discussing sex, violence, what happened between men and women . . . about so many experiences that the women I knew in the early 1970s were beginning to reveal. Friends reluctantly talked about abuse by husbands and boyfriends, about dates where they were forced to have sex, and about many years filled with shame. These stories deeply affected me, and suddenly, with a new perspective, I looked at my own experiences: groped on the subway as I grew up in New York, coerced to have sex with a professor, sexually humiliated by a boyfriend, and *always afraid,* as were all of the women in my family. I realized how much I had resented and resisted the restrictions and fear arising from the unspoken dangers that lurked everywhere for girls. These realizations changed my life forever. I discovered that my private shame and fear were not mine alone. Something far greater and more powerful affected me as a woman, and it was complicated further by my ethnic and religious culture and my family's generations of poverty.

I was a social worker, a mother with young daughters. I had visions of organizing people and communities to advocate for social justice, for a future without poverty or violence. When women I knew were raped and not taken seriously, I was outraged, and along with others in the growing women's movement, took action to launch one of the first rape hotlines in the United States.

Since then, I have been passionately committed to stopping the pervasiveness and brutality of violence against women. In my journey I have played many roles: I've worked with survivors, social justice and women's movement leaders, professionals, and volunteers to launch a shelter for battered women and their children. I've run advocacy, violence prevention, and mental health programs in several organizations, always trying to reach out to and empower women and girls. I've been committed to bringing diverse people together to make communities stronger and safer for women and children, and I've organized and developed a powerful regional coalition and a network of local organizations. I have trained adults, educated youth, and counseled women and girls.

Speaking to high school students about preventing sexual assault and domestic violence in the early 1980s gave me hope that the next generation of women and girls would not have to suffer from these horrible experiences. I was shocked when girls talked to me not about their parents' experiences, as I'd been expecting, but about their own. I discovered that girls as young as thirteen were being beaten and emotionally abused in the same ways that adult women were. They were dating, not married; living with parents, not independently; surrounded by friends and families, attending school, but isolated in their intimate relationships. At that time, no one recognized the serious danger of teen dating violence.

My daughters were teenagers at that time—I was especially aware of teens' culture and vulnerabilities. I trained people who work with youth and wrote books for professionals, teens, and parents. I spoke to any audience that would listen and appeared on many television and radio shows.

My favorite audience for the past twenty-five years has been my students at UCLA, where I teach graduate courses on mental health policies, including issues for women, and undergraduate women's studies courses on violence against women. Many students take these classes to learn more about their personal experiences with violence, and many go on after graduation to contribute to social change and empowerment of women. Whatever one has experienced, even if never exposed to violence, studying violence against women is always both personal and academic.

Through all of these years, I have admired and been inspired by the resilience and courage of the women and girls I have known as they overcome seemingly insurmountable obstacles. I have kept a vow I made to tell their stories of sexual, emotional, and physical violence—and what I have learned from them. That vow has guided everything I have done, including writing this book, so you, too, can learn about what they have faced and overcome.

I am proud of the changes and successes of the past thirty years. So many women and children now live free from violence, and they have options for preventing or escaping and recovering from it. But I still feel profoundly frightened, powerless, and angry at the pervasiveness and injustice of violence against women—it continues to be common and accepted as "the way things are." As I write this, hundreds of girls in Sierra Leone and Eastern Congo are trying to recover from being brutally raped as part of armed conflict in their countries. Girls from Southeast Asia and Central America are enslaved in domestic and sex work in Bangkok and Japan—and Los Angeles. In my neighborhood recently, several women and teenage girls sought help to get out of abusive relationships, a girl was gang-raped at a fraternity party, and a young immigrant woman had her newborn baby taken away from her because of the baby's father's violent threats.

There is still great urgency for women and men to learn about, speak out against, and take action to end the violence that continues to be widespread against women and girls. The actions, big and small, of thousands of people like you and me, worldwide, have sustained an ever-growing groundswell of protest and change, and empowerment and relief from shame for individual survivors. Major campaigns to change international policies, such as those of Human Rights Watch and Amnesty International, and individual one-on-one efforts to prevent violence are equally essential for social change. I have been inspired by the hard work that is now dedicated to stopping violence:

by my students who organize the Clothesline Project, the Take Back the Night march, and the antitrafficking Polaris Project on campus; by students who educate boys and girls about rape prevention; and by others who lobby in Washington DC for human rights and violence prevention legislation. I'm encouraged when students discuss the realities of violence against women with everyone they know, changing attitudes in their own families and communities. I hope that reading this book will inspire you to continue to study—and take action to prevent—future violence against women and girls.

Women practicing self-defense. © Barrie Levy

CHAPTER 1

VIOLENCE AGAINST WOMEN: AN OVERVIEW

VIOLENCE AGAINST WOMEN SURROUNDS all of us, whether or not we are aware of it. Think about the small decisions you make every day. If you are a woman, when you decide what to wear, where to go, how to get there, what time of day you are outdoors, and what affects your sense of security and safety, are you aware that you are afraid of being sexually assaulted? If you are a man, when you think about your mother, sister, girlfriend, or wife, and their activities and acquaintances, are you aware of your urge to protect them or your anger at them because of your fear that they could be sexually assaulted? If you are a woman who has experienced or witnessed violence, how has this affected your daily decisions?

"Not all women live in constant fear," writes London Metropolitan University professor Liz Kelly in her 1988 book *Surviving Sexual Violence,* "but many of women's routine decisions and behavior are almost automatic measures taken to protect themselves from potential sexual violence." The effects of violence against women are experienced not only by individual survivors, but by their communities, and by the women, men, and children who care about them. Kelly's comments highlight a powerful fact about violence against women all over the world: it affects everyone.

Violence against women is widespread in every country and society. It is so common that some experts consider it a "normal" aspect of women's experiences. Some studies estimate that half of the women in the United States have been sexually harassed at some time in their lives. Other studies show that almost half of women worldwide

1

Sexual Terrorism

Author Carole Sheffield describes her experience of an "ordinary" event in the following excerpt from her 1997 essay "Sexual Terrorism":

One afternoon I collected my laundry and went to a nearby Laundromat. . . . After I had loaded and started the machines, I became acutely aware of my environment. It was just after 6:00 PM and dark, the other stores were closed, the Laundromat was brightly lit, and my car was the only one in the lot. Anyone passing by could readily see that I was alone and isolated. Knowing that rape is often a crime of opportunity, I became terrified. I wanted to leave and find a Laundromat that was busier, but my clothes were well into the wash cycle, and, besides, I felt I was being "silly," "paranoid." The feeling of terror persisted, so I sat in my car, windows up and doors locked. When the wash was completed, I dashed in, threw the clothes into the dryer, and ran back out to my car. When the clothes were dry, I tossed them recklessly into the basket and hurriedly drove away to fold them in the security of my home.

Although I was not victimized in a direct, physical way or by objective or measurable standards, I felt victimized. It was, for me, a terrifying experience. I felt controlled by an invisible force. I was angry that something as commonplace as doing laundry after a day's work jeopardized my well-being. Mostly I was angry at being unfree: a hostage of a culture that, for the most part, encourages violence against females, instructs men in the methodology of sexual violence, and provides them with ready justification for their violence. I was angry that I could be victimized by being "in the wrong place at the wrong time." The essence of terrorism is that one never knows when is the wrong time and where is the wrong place.

have experienced domestic violence. Violence can happen to anyone, although some people are more vulnerable or more affected than others. This book aims to answer your questions about why women's fear of violence—particularly sexual violence—is so common and powerful, and why some women and communities are more vulnerable to violence than others.

Violence against women is complicated. It is difficult to study, and research results about it are inconsistent. There is no truly objective way to think about the issue—values, beliefs, and emotions affect how we see it, or if we see it at all. Violent perpetrators are motivated by a complex range of factors: psychological, familial, economic, political, environmental, and social. Social structures that maintain the status quo of centuries of women's low status, even as these societies undergo change, are a powerful force in legitimizing violence against women and making it invisible. This book provides an overview of the multiple dimensions that interact with one another to make violence so common in women's lives, in the United States and globally, and so difficult to eradicate. Violence against women inflicts tremendous costs and consequences in all countries and societies.

Wonderful changes have taken place in the last thirty years. Violence against women is no longer as hidden or misunderstood as it was. Empowered individual women have made the transition from "victim" to "survivor" of violence. Activists all over the world have been remarkably effective in challenging the status quo and developing safe havens for victims. Governments and international bodies have passed laws, treaties, and policies for prevention and intervention. Activists, researchers, governments, and international bodies have committed a great deal of effort to define concepts and acts related to violence against women so that language and perceptions match realities.

Defining the Issue

According to Liz Kelly, violence against women involves "behavior that is violent, uses physical force or threat, [and] is intimidating, coercive, [or] damaging to women"; it includes "physical, visual, verbal or sexual

4 WOMEN AND VIOLENCE

acts that are experienced by a woman or girl at the time or later as a threat, invasion or assault" and acts "that have the effect of hurting or degrading her and/or taking away her ability to control contact (intimate or otherwise) with another individual."

Many writers and experts use Kelly's definition because it has important elements regarding the realities of violence against women. First, it defines as violent a *range of different kinds of behavior* that include coercion and emotional abuse. Second, these behaviors are recognized as *harmful as experienced by the woman or girl,* even if they are not recognized as such by others whose perspectives may not reflect actual experiences of women and girls. Third, it focuses on *the effect* of the behavior on the victim, rather than on the intentions or perceptions of the perpetrator. Fourth, it emphasizes the effect of *taking away a woman's ability to control contact* with another person, which is a major aspect of violence against women as a social problem.

The United Nations' 1993 *Declaration on the Elimination of Violence Against Women* defines violence against women as "any act of gender-based violence that results in or is likely to result in physical, sexual or psychological harm or suffering to women, including threats of such acts, coercion or arbitrary deprivations of liberty, whether occurring in public or private life." Among the many acts this declaration explicitly covers are marital rape, sexual abuse of female children, sexual harassment, trafficking in women, forced prostitution, and violence perpetrated by the state (such as rape used as a weapon in war).

The UN definition is important because it focuses on the responsibility of the state to address the human rights of women, and it recognizes violence against women as gender based and both public and private. It is significant to challenge the view that violence against women is only an individual, private problem of a particular victim; it's also important to recognize that this violence is institutionalized and supported by the state. We see violence as "institutionalized" when it is justified as normal or acceptable by institutions such as religions, legal systems, workplaces, and government policies.

The following sections cover the most common types of violence that women face in homes, in public places, and in workplaces: intimate partner violence, sexual assault, and sexual harassment.

Intimate Partner Violence

Intimate partner violence occurs when a person uses force or the threat of force to gain control in an intimate heterosexual or same-sex relationship. It is prevalent in all societies and across cultures, and although some men are abused in relationships with women, women are the predominant victims of intimate partner violence. Perpetrators may be current or former boyfriends, husbands, or girlfriends; couples dating while living apart, cohabiting, or married; people who share children or do not; young and elder people.

Intimate partner violence is complex and multidimensional; it includes physical and sexual abuse, stalking, and psychological/emotional abuse. *Physical abuse* refers to any act of physical aggression, such as shoving, throwing objects, beating, burning, or assault with a weapon. *Sexual abuse* refers to any sexual act that a woman or girl submits to against her will because of force, threat of force, or coercion, without consenting or without the ability to consent. It can include sexual exploitation involving sexual contact with others against a woman's will. It includes sexual control of reproductive rights and any form of sexual manipulation carried out by a perpetrator who intends (or is perceived to intend) to cause emotional, sexual, and physical degradation to another person. It includes repeatedly using demeaning sexual language, minimizing or ignoring a partner's feelings about sex, or making humiliating comments about a partner's body.

Defining "consent" or "use of force" in the context of an intimate relationship is often more confusing than when sexual assault is committed by strangers or acquaintances; many women don't label as sexual abuse or rape their experiences of having sex when they don't want to but are too frightened to say no, or their experiences of being forced to have sex with someone with whom they have an intimate relationship.

Stalking is defined by the Office for Victims of Crime as "the willful or intentional commission of a series of acts that would cause a reasonable person to fear death or serious bodily injury and that, in fact, does place the victim in fear of death or serious bodily injury." Stalkers are often former intimate partners continuing to try to exercise control by being punishing, intimidating, and frightening. They engage in harassment and threats, surveillance activities, and/or vandalism repeatedly over long periods.

Psychological or emotional abuse takes place in abusive relationships whether or not the abuser uses physical violence. Christian Molidor and Richard Tolman are researchers who have identified and categorized several major types of psychological abuse; these have been observed in teen as well as adult relationships and include:

- *isolation or monopolization:* actions an abuser takes to make himself the center of a woman's life—for example, expressing jealous rages that result in her restricting her time with friends and family; checking up on her by calling constantly when she is with others; following her; or making urgent and threatening but ultimately unnecessary demands for her attention when she is at work or with others.

- *economic abuse:* controlling money, spending, and/or a woman's ability to work—for example, taking her money and not leaving her enough to manage; controlling her spending by restricting her access to their money; not allowing her to shop alone; cruelly criticizing her financial decisions; or interfering with her work or studies by showing up, calling constantly, harassing her, or creating conflicts that frighten or distract her.

- *degradation and humiliation:* undermining a woman's self-esteem by shaming her, criticizing or mocking her in front of others, or forcing her do things that she finds humiliating.

- *rigid sex-role expectations:* asserting that masculinity justifies abuse—for example, believing that an abuser has a right to express his anger and that a woman is obliged to "take it" if he needs her to; asserting his entitlement to discipline her, punish her, and "keep her in line"; or expecting that he is entitled to do what he wants as the "master" in his own family.

- *psychological destabilization:* making a woman feel crazy and stupid—for example, manipulating her so she doesn't know the truth; cruelly twisting what she says or does to give it an unintended and crazy meaning; or, after she implements a joint decision, attacking her for doing it, stating that she is stupid and the action is not what he told her to do.
- *withholding emotional caring and nurturance:* alternating loving and cruel, nurturing and punishing behavior to keep a woman in denial about the abuse and hopeful that if she gets everything "right" the abuser will be caring and nurturing.

Some survivors of psychological abuse describe their experience as "brainwashing." They describe their abusers as unleashing unbearable verbal attacks and rages; restricting their activities outside the relationship; relentlessly criticizing them; expressing extreme jealousy; endlessly interrogating them and accusing them of infidelity; deliberately isolating them by alienating them from friends and family and demanding exclusive attention; and manipulating them so that they feel crazy and doubt their own perceptions. Psychological abuse undermines women's self-esteem and sense of having a valued identity. Many women find that emotional abuse is worse than physical abuse and causes longer-lasting damage.

Abusers use physically and emotionally abusive behaviors that are referred to as patterns of *coercive control.* The abusive nature of the relationship exists all the time, even outside of physically violent incidents. Evan Stark, an award-winning researcher and professor of health administration, refers to coercive control in his book, *Coercive Control: How Men Entrap Women in Personal Life,* as "a course of calculated, malevolent conduct deployed almost exclusively by men to dominate individual women by interweaving repeated physical abuse with three equally important tactics: intimidation, isolation and control." Stark compares coercive control to "capture crimes" such as kidnapping, with the twist that its power is based in sexist norms: "[L]ike hostages, victims of coercive control are frequently deprived of money, food, access to communication or transportation and other survival resources even as they are cut off from family, friends and other supports. But unlike other capture crimes it relies for its impact on women's vulnerabilities as women due to sexual inequality. The main means used to establish control is the microregulation of everyday behaviors associated with stereotypic female roles, such as how women dress, cook, clean, socialize or perform sexually."

Domestic violence researcher Michael Johnson made an important contribution to understanding multiple patterns of intimate partner violence by distinguishing between two distinct types: "situational couple violence" and "intimate terrorism." *Situational couple violence* occurs when day-to-day conflicts occasionally get out of hand, leading to minor forms of violence. Couples who experience it usually lack conflict resolution skills; it is likely to be mutual, and it may be initiated by either partner. The violence can be a serious problem in terms of its impact on a couple or family, but it is substantially different from intimate terrorism.

Intimate terrorism, on the other hand, is the repeated and ongoing use of abusive tactics and physical force to obtain (and maintain) power and control over an intimate partner. Through time, the abusive behavior induces fear and subservience in the victim, as well as causing chronic injury and trauma. The perpetrator weaves violence through the "normal" interactions of daily life in a way that may make it difficult for a woman to clearly identify the beginning and end of any particular violent episode. Because it is a regular occurrence in a woman's life, it is more disruptive and harmful to victims (including children who witness it) and society. Many physically abused women experience physical violence on a regular basis.

Researchers Patricia Mahoney, Linda Williams, and Carolyn West point out several particular characteristics of battering relationships, or relationships in which intimate terrorism takes place, that are important to understand. Battering relationships are ongoing and similar to nonbattering relationships, they explain: couples share intimacy, affection, families, and history. Although abuse may occur throughout the relationship, there are often many ways in which the couple enjoy being together and value or need one another. Both partners may feel love for one another and want to protect each other from harm, which makes battering unlike any other kind of interpersonal violence. Another difference from other kinds of violence is that the perpetrator knows his partner intimately, so he often knows how to hurt her. Therefore, the victim is unsafe even if they don't live together, or if they are no longer together. Abuse often continues after the relationship ends.

Both partners are likely to believe that the abused woman is responsible for the violence. When others blame the victim for provoking the violence through her behavior or by staying or returning, they contribute to her entrapment. They overlook her efforts to be safe and survive without understanding the reality of the threat or how difficult it is to leave the relationship because of the complex ways the abuser makes it impossible for her to survive independently from him.

Intimate partner violence is as prevalent in same-sex relationships as it is in heterosexual relationships. The kinds of abusive behavior and the dynamics are similar. The primary difference is the context in which it occurs—that is, the environment of feared, perceived, or real homophobia and heterosexism and the ways these are internalized and institutionalized. Not all people in same-sex relationships identify themselves as lesbian, gay, or bisexual, but issues faced by LGB people arise for them as well. Same-sex partner violence is often understood as gendered, in that abusers often attack aspects of a partner that are perceived as feminine.

The abuser may use homophobia to control his or her partner by threatening to expose or out the victim at work or to family. Another control tactic involves demeaning or humiliating the victim based on the victim's struggles with her or his own sexuality. The same-sex couple may be more isolated than heterosexual couples if they are not open about their relationship and their personal lives are hidden from those around them. They may have an intense bond that is based on their dependence on one another and on the feeling that they have

Teen Relationship Violence

Violence in intimate relationships takes place at all ages. Women ages sixteen to twenty-four experience the highest rates of intimate violence in the United States. Some facts about college students and dating violence:

- 21 percent of college students report they have experienced dating violence by a current partner; 32 percent report dating violence by a previous partner. (Sellers and Bromley, 1996.)
- More than 13 percent of college women report they have been stalked during one school year. Of these, 42 percent were stalked by a current or former boyfriend. (Fisher, Cullen, and Turner, 2000.)
- 60 percent of acquaintance rapes of college women occur in casual or steady dating relationships. (Johnson and Sigler, 1996.)
- Younger college students, especially freshmen, experience more sexual violence than older students, most likely from a dating partner or acquaintance.
- Among college women who described an experience meeting the legal definition of rape, less than half defined the experience as rape. (Fisher, Cullen, and Turner, 2000.)

Although the kinds of violence they experience are the same as those experienced by adult women, high school and college-age girls are vulnerable to relationship violence because of factors that are unique to their age group, such as:

- The major transitions in their lives, exposing them to a variety of social expectations and pressures for which they may be unprepared
- Newly gained independence from parents
- Relative inexperience with sexual relationships
- Pressure to conform, to be in a relationship
- Likelihood (more than adults) to interpret abusive behavior, control, and jealousy as signs of love about their friends' as well as their own relationships, along with romanticized, dramatic views of love
- Limited experience advocating for their own health, safety, and well-being, and reluctance to seek help from adults

a shared enemy in the homophobic world around them. The abused partner may become determined to keep the violence hidden because of the perceived double stigma of being in a same-sex and an abusive relationship. Gay, lesbian, and bisexual communities have tended to deny that abuse or violence takes place to protect themselves against negative attitudes and because of the erroneous belief that women and gay men are never violent.

Although services for lesbian, gay, bisexual, and transgender abusers and abused partners exist in cities such as Los Angeles, New York, and San Francisco, access to safe and supportive help is limited. Victims who seek aid from law enforcement, health services, or other agencies may experience secondary victimization—that is, they may find that they are not taken seriously, have their sexual orientation exposed against their will, or be treated with insensitivity, encountering homophobic or transphobic attitudes or abusive behavior from the people who are supposed to help. Secondary victimization leads to more isolation and hopelessness about being safe or strong enough to deal with the situation.

Sexual Assault

The defining characteristic of sexual assault is that it involves lack of choice or consent. Sociologists and advocates use the term "sexual assault" to encompass a wide range of unwanted sexual acts in various contexts, involving coercion and deception as well as force. Legally, rape is one form of sexual assault, although in common language the terms are sometimes used interchangeably—despite the fact that sexual assault also encompasses other criminal acts (such as molestation).

There are several types of rape: acquaintance, date, stranger, and marital rape. Well-known sexual assault researcher Mary Koss and her colleagues offer a concise legal definition of rape in their book *No Safe Haven: Male Violence Against Women at Home, at Work, and in the Community*, stating that it involves "nonconsensual sexual penetration . . . obtained by physical force, by threat of bodily harm or at such time when the victim is incapable of giving consent by virtue of mental illness, mental retardation or intoxication." They define sexual penetration as "sexual intercourse, cunnilingus, fellatio, anal intercourse, or any other intrusion, however slight, of any part of a person's body," but they specify that it doesn't necessarily include male ejaculation.

Rape is a gendered crime. The vast majority of rapes are perpetrated by men against women. Even when sexual orientation is taken into account, researchers have found that whether one is male or female, the primary risk factor for acquaintance rape is dating men. A significant, fairly recent recognition of women's right to refuse sex is reflected in laws passed in most U.S. states during the 1990s against marital rape; before this, sex forced by a woman's husband was not recognized as rape because his right to demand sex was assumed to be part of marriage.

Extensive research on rape during the past thirty years has shown that rape is prevalent all over the world, that it is one of the most underreported crimes, and that the majority of rapes and attempted rapes are committed by someone known to the victim. Rape is difficult to count: rates vary according to the methods used to measure rape and who is in the samples. Researchers have estimated that among industrialized societies 21 percent to 27 percent of women experience rape at some point in their lives, compared with 43 percent and 90 percent in nonindustrial societies. Rape rates are especially high for young women between twelve and thirty-five. According to a Department of Justice study, thirty-five of every one thousand women who attend colleges or universities experience an attempted or completed rape each year.

Acquaintance rape is far more common than stranger rape and is often a hidden crime. Victims often don't label their experiences of rape as such, yet they often suffer from the health, educational, social, and mental health problems that result from rape. Because of erroneous beliefs, they may not define as rape such experiences as coerced sex, forced sex with someone they know, or forced sex with someone with whom they may have at some point had consensual sex.

Many of these erroneous beliefs are based on social and cultural expectations of masculinity and femininity, and of men's and women's roles in relationships. Sexual aggression is often viewed as normal, a part of dating, and not serious ("Boys will be boys"). Young women are socialized to accept responsibility for controlling sexual interactions with men and to assume blame for their own sexual victimization ("What did she do to make him rape her?" or "Girls have to expect that all guys want the same thing"). Young men are socialized to ignore women's attempts to resist sexual advances because they see a woman's "no" as a game. Surveys of young people reveal that there are circumstances in which they believe that forced sex is justifiable—for example, if a girl goes to a guy's home, if he pays for dinner, or if she "leads him on."

Internationally, rape and other forms of sexual violence—gang rape, abduction for rape or prostitution, sexual slavery, forced marriage, and sexual mutilation—are defined as torture and war crimes under the Geneva Convention, and as war crimes and crimes against humanity by the International Criminal Court (ICC). The ICC's 1998 Rome Statute defines these crimes as situations in which the woman is deprived of her ability to consent to sex—which includes providing sex to avoid harm or obtain basic necessities. Sexual violence may be committed as a widespread or systematic attack against a civilian population, and in some cases it may be an element of "ethnic cleansing" or genocide. Rape in war deliberately aims to destroy bonds of family and society and to demoralize the enemy. Women and children are considered "spoils of war"; rape humiliates defeated armies by violating their families and "property."

Sexual Harassment

Although women have been subjected to sexual demands to keep their jobs for centuries, the term "sexual harassment" was coined in the United States only recently. Catharine MacKinnon's 1979 book, *Sexual Harassment of Working Women: A Case of Sex Discrimination,* provided the first basis upon which workplace sexual harassment could be challenged legally—as a form of discrimination based on gender. A brilliant legal advocate for women's rights, MacKinnon made a case for legal sanctions against sexual harassment as discrimination and a violation of civil rights. Legal consequences for workplace sexual harassment had eluded reformers who focused on criminal law because many of the behaviors that constitute harassment are not defined as criminal acts in state penal codes. Moving the issue into civil rather than criminal jurisdictions gave women a venue in which they could successfully pursue justice. For this reason, social and legal changes regarding sexual harassment have taken place through civil sex discrimination cases in which companies and schools have been sued for damages; many lower court decisions have been appealed in higher courts. Changes have been made through landmark higher court rulings that have legitimized and clarified sexual harassment law, and financially punished offending companies, rather than through changes in the criminal justice system.

The Equal Employment Opportunity Commission and the U.S. Office of Civil Rights define workplace and educational "sexual harassment" as any form of uninvited sexual attention that either explicitly or implicitly becomes a condition of one's work or one's educational experiences. Victims often have no recourse other than quitting or changing jobs or schools, which is a significant factor in women's job turnover and slower career advancement, and it therefore sustains the gender gap in pay.

MacKinnon conceptualized two forms of workplace sexual harassment: quid pro quo harassment and the creation of a hostile environment. Quid pro quo involves the exchange of sexual favors for special employment treatment. Those who refuse risk punishment, such as demotion, dismissal, or denial of basic necessities for doing their jobs. It is usually perpetrated by a person with the power to hire, promote, or assign benefits.

Hostile environments are created in workplaces where sexualized talk and behavior are experienced by some as demeaning and humiliating, affecting their work. The behavior may or may not target an individual, but it differs from quid pro quo sexual harassment because there is no exchange of favors, reward for participation, or punishment for refusing. Studies have shown that hostile climates are created in organizations with values supporting or allowing gender inequality and hostility against women.

Almost every study of sexual harassment has found substantial differences between men and women in their responses, attitudes, and beliefs. Women are significantly more likely than men to react to men's sexualized behavior in study scenarios as harassing, offensive, and threatening, especially in more subtle situations (for example, repeatedly asking a woman out after she has made it clear she's not interested) and hostile environments. This research has led to the establishment of the "reasonable woman" standard as the legal basis for determining whether sexual harassment has occurred. In *Ellison v Brady* (1991), the U.S. 9th Circuit Court ruled that the law must take into account the victim's perspective of the harasser's behavior, stating that "conduct that many men consider unobjectionable may offend many women."

The difference between men's and women's perspectives of harassing behavior became apparent in the intense media and public debates about Anita Hill's testimony at Senate hearings to confirm Clarence Thomas's appointment to the U.S. Supreme Court in 1991. Hill claimed that Thomas had sexually harassed her when he was her supervisor at the Equal Employment Opportunity Commission. Many men believed she was overreacting to an insignificant experience, and many women identified with the insidious harmful effects of her experience. Regardless of people's responses, there is little doubt that the hearings raised national awareness of the problem: sexual harassment reports doubled during the three-year period after the hearings.

Hill's testimony also revealed differences between white and African American perspectives. Some debates focused on the exposure of an African American man to public scrutiny about sexual behavior, making the point that white men are not subjected to such scrutiny. Kimberlé Crenshaw's essay on the controversy, "Whose Story Is It Anyway? Feminist and Antiracist Appropriations of Anita Hill," examined the issue from a feminist of color's perspective. As Crenshaw explains, Thomas evoked the experience of racism by claiming that he was being "lynched," and he succeeded in overpowering Hill's allegations and discrediting her. Meanwhile, Hill's credibility was threatened by the history, dating to the slavery era, of sexualization of African American women's bodies. Because of her status as both African American and a woman, and Thomas's status as African American, Hill's claims didn't fall tidily into such conventional categories as racism *or* sexual harassment, because she was harassed based on gender *and* race; thus Hill was a victim of compounded vulnerabilities.

Workplace sexual harassment is common; estimates are that it may affect as many as one out of every two women during the course of their working lives. Not all women are equally at risk: young, single, and divorced women are significantly more likely to be victimized than older married women. And harassment based on race *and* gender is more common and qualitatively different as a form of discrimination than gender discrimination alone. For example, in October 2007, the Los Angeles Fire Department was charged by the federal Equal Employment Opportunity Commission following an investigation that showed "a pattern and practice of harassment and retaliation exists for . . . female and black firefighters based on gender and race." The fire department had not responded to complaints by two female firefighters, one Latina and the other black, that they had suffered unfair discipline and retaliation after complaining of sexually explicit remarks, unwanted touching, and excessive training designed to run them out of the department, and that they subsequently had been denied transfer requests and promotions because of race and gender. And a survey of a random sample of 126 African American and 122 Caucasian women residents of L.A. County indicated that 67 percent of African American (compared with 45 percent of Caucasian women) reported having been propositioned in the workplace. The term "sexual harassment" and research about it, while useful, are still limited: they do not adequately account for violations that are also homophobic or racist.

Examining the Causes of Violence Against Women

Many perspectives try to explain the causes of violence against women.

Here is an overview of some of the major ones; bear in mind that many researchers who study violence against women have concluded that no one approach adequately explains the phenomenon. The perspectives are divided into two categories: individual, focusing on causes of violent behavior unique to individuals; and sociocultural, focusing on the influences of society and culture. A combination of multiple factors, from both of these types of perspectives, actually best explains what is known about the causes of violence against women.

Individual Perspectives

The most popular individual-focused perspectives are the *social learning theories,* which explain violent behavior as learned from one's environment. According to these theories, individuals learn how to behave from their exposure to and experiences of violence. When they observe or imitate behavior, they learn what those around them consider appropriate. Boys are most likely to imitate fathers, and girls to imitate mothers, through the socialization processes that take place in families. When their behavior is responded to and reinforced, they become conditioned to continue the behavior. This process is responsible for the *intergenerational transmission of violence,* in which violence against women is learned from one generation to the next. Violence is learned as a tactic for getting what one wants or expressing emotions.

Social learning theories have provided a valuable perspective on the complex issue of the influence on children of exposure to violence in the community and in the media as well as in the family. This exposure—along with other factors, but not by itself—is recognized to have had a significant impact on the behavior of people who later use violence. But critics of social learning theories say that they don't explain much of the phenomenon of violence against women. The notion of children as passive learners who do what they see and respond only to conditioning is not supported by child development research. It is also too simplistic a view of the many kinds of dynamics within families that influence children's learning and behavior. Although studies of people who perpetrate violence or abuse indicate that witnessing violence is an important risk factor—in other words, people who use violent behavior are more likely than those who don't to have been exposed to violence during childhood—most people who were abused or who witnessed violence as a child do not grow up to be violent, nor do they become victims of violence. Also, the correlation between witnessing violence and becoming a victim of it is low—it is estimated that about 30 percent of adult female victims witnessed violence or abuse as children.

Intergenerational patterns of violence can also be attributed to other kinds of environmental influences on children and their later behavior as adults. Recent studies have identified the transmission of attitudes from parents to children as significant: for example, attitudes about how men treat women or about circumstances in which aggressive behavior is justified.

One of the most important explanations for violence that stems from childhood exposure to violence in the home comes from studies that focus on *trauma*—specifically, the traumatic effects on children of witnessing abuse or violence. Rather than experiencing a cognitive, learning process, children may respond to violence by undergoing a series of physical and emotional changes in the process of attempting to cope with overactive stress responses and ongoing traumatic stress reactions. They may manifest hypervigilance, hypersensitivity, increased startle responses, dissociation, nightmares, and serious distractability; most relevantly, they may too easily perceive danger and threat in situations that most others do not view the same way. Post-traumatic stress is identified in the histories of many people who use violent behavior.

It is commonly believed that individuals who are violent toward women are not solely influenced by their childhood environments but have *mental disorders or personality disorders*, and so they don't have normal inhibitions that stop them from using violence. Some violence is committed by people with antisocial (sociopathic) disorders, who have no sense of conscience, remorse, or empathy with the victim or concern about the consequences of their actions. There is evidence that some people who use violent behavior may be depressed, bipolar, obsessive, or narcissistic. Donald Dutton, who has counseled and studied men who abuse their intimate partners, identifies in these men patterns of what he calls "borderline personality organization," which has some of the features of borderline personality disorder but occurs only in the intimate relationship and not in other arenas of the batterer's life. Men who assault women have been found to have greater needs for power than men who do not assault women. It is possible that men who have low self-esteem or who feel little control over others or the events in their lives are more likely to feel powerless, which may lead them to attempt to control or punish women.

Critics of these psychopathological explanations of violence against women are concerned that psychological problems are often used as an excuse for violent behavior, minimizing the deliberate nature of abusive behavior and the perpetrator's responsibility for his actions. Also, there is no consistent pattern of psychopathology in studies of batterers or rapists. Psychological patterns such as obsessiveness or borderline personality organization may be difficult to distinguish from intentional emotional manipulation and control. The overwhelming majority of people who have the psychological problems suspected of causing violence against women do not abuse or rape women. Therefore, some factor or factors must combine with these problems or disorders to cause violence against women.

Biological and physiological explanations consider men's use of aggressive or violent behavior toward women as part of the process of natural selection. In one example of this thinking, since the goal for males is to reproduce as much as possible to increase the chance of passing on their genes, rape can be seen as an extreme response to natural selection pressure.

The use of *alcohol,* commonly associated with violent behavior, is consistently found in many of the profiles of abusive men and is linked to rape. There is also a link between drug abuse and violence. Although victims, abusers, and rapists often believe that alcohol or drugs cause the violence, experts believe that people use alcohol and drugs to reduce their inhibitions about hurting others and are very likely to become violent with or without getting drunk or high.

Sociocultural Perspectives

Sociocultural theories explain violence against women as stemming from social structures or cultural conditions. Advocates of these theories say that men abuse women "because they can." They mean that in our society men who are inclined to abuse women for any number of personal reasons find it easy to justify it and get away with it without being punished or stopped.

Family structure perspectives focus on family violence in particular, arguing that women are as violent as men in relationships and families. According to well-known family violence researcher Murray Straus, the origin of the problem is in the nature of the family structure. Violence in U.S. families is often considered legitimate: many parents spank their children or accept sibling violence as inevitable. Aggressive, abusive, and violent behavior is defended as within the range of normal in all relationships in the family. Solutions to the problem of family violence lie in challenging these attitudes about violence as normal and identifying them as harmful and unacceptable.

Critics believe that this perspective ignores the power and status differences between men and women, arguing that men's use of violence is not the same as women's. Family structure perspectives do not make distinctions among the patterns, contexts, or motivations for use of violence, and therefore they may not present an accurate picture of the effects of violence. They also approach violence as resulting from conflict between family members, which ignores commonly seen patterns of coercive control. The value of this perspective, however, is that it addresses social norms that tolerate and therefore allow violent and aggressive behavior within the family and in intimate relationships.

Cultural acceptance of violence is high in the United States. Societies that reinforce the use of violence as a legitimate means to achieve desired ends support violence against women. Although this does address cultural tolerance for and glorification of violence, this explanation, however, is criticized as not explaining why only some men use violent behavior against women.

Some see *stress* as a risk factor for family violence. When individuals or groups face stressors they cannot manage—for instance, poverty, discrimination, immigration problems, community crises, personal difficulties, or medical problems—the resulting stress has the potential to lead to violent behavior.

Feminist theory focuses on power, on gender, and on the structure of relationships in a male-dominated, patriarchal culture. According to feminist theory, the main factors that contribute to violence against women include historically male-dominated social structures and socialization practices teaching men and women gender-specific roles. Feminists have analyzed dynamics of oppression and the intersection of gender, race, and class to explain that the institutionalization of violence against women in political, legal, and economic systems makes it invisible and acceptable. Feminist research has focused on women's stories of their own survival, victimization, and fears as the major source of information about gendered violence, and it has confronted gender bias in research that reflects patriarchal social attitudes.

Feminist theories have been criticized for an exclusive, too-simplistic focus on gender. Violence against women is too complex to be understood only as a problem of gender. Gender roles—and sexism and racism embedded in social structures—are powerful components of male violence toward women, but other factors contribute as well, and multiple dimensions interact with one another to make it complex, difficult to explain, and difficult to eradicate. This book emphasizes the complexity of these interacting factors and uses the analysis of social structural power dynamics related to gender, race, and class inherent in feminist theory as a guiding principle—not to oversimplify, but rather to account for complex social environments that perpetuate and influence individual acts of violence.

Multidimensional Perspectives

Multidimensional explanations of violence against women integrate social factors, such as class, gender, and culture, with individual characteristics, such as family history, psychopathology, and alcohol or drug use. Reluctance of institutions to intervene, cultural approval of violence, and social constructions of "masculinity" contribute additional dimensions. These theories view violence against women as complex, with individual and social factors combining to cause and perpetuate the problem.

Violence as a Manifestation of Institutionalized Sexism

Many feminists attribute the pervasiveness of violence against women to *institutionalized sexism*—cultural norms and expectations that (among other things) accept women as "legitimate victims" of male violence. In general, cultural norms and expectations prescribe and proscribe the rights and responsibilities (i.e., the roles) of all people in a particular social status or category. They are learned and transmitted from one generation to the next in the home, workplace, and in peer groups. In most societies, norms related to gender and violence support female subordination and justify male violence. They pervade legal systems, literature, media, and everyday discourse. Nilda Rimonte, founder of the Center for the Pacific Asian Family in Los Angeles, defines "legitimate victims" as individuals seen as having little or no reason to complain about their victimization because they belong to an inferior social class. Their social status justifies their victimization— they deserve punishment (a perspective expressed in common responses such as "She must have asked for it").

Although most men do not maintain these attitudes or use aggressive behaviors toward women, the cultural norms in the United States and worldwide create a remarkable social tolerance for violent behavior in the family or toward certain women. What makes this clear is that beating, emotional torture, and sexual violation are unquestionably intolerable and unacceptable if committed by a stranger or by one man toward another. A well-known study simulated a scene of a man yelling at and hitting a woman on a public walkway with many people passing by. When anyone approached to help, the man said, "She's my wife," and passersby backed away and did nothing to help. Teenage girls have reported that fights between boys in school or in public get an immediate response from authorities, whereas violent incidents against girls, occurring in view of others, get no response at all. A small percentage of cases of rape and battering are actually prosecuted, and convictions are rare compared to the numbers of reports made to law enforcement and compared to the consequences for stranger assault in the United States and worldwide.

Several specific societal dynamics operate together to enforce the legitimacy and acceptability of violence against women as a means to control women as a class.

Cultural myths blame victims for their victimization, view domestic violence as a private matter, eroticize and excuse male violence, fail to hold men accountable, and trivialize the real consequences of violence for women, whether directly victimized or not.

Sexual scripts, a concept introduced by psychologist Sandra Bem, reflect androcentric heterosexuality (a heterosexual perspective that views males and male experiences as the norm), eroticize sexual inequality, and support male domination as normal and natural. In these "scripts," men objectify women, emphasizing their physical attractiveness and ability to stimulate and satisfy men's desires, rather than seeing women as human beings like themselves.

Gender and gender related social roles define masculinity and femininity as clusters of traits that depend on what is considered masculine in societies and cultural groups. An example is the belief that men are dominant, strong, and "in charge," and that women are passive, irrational, weak, and submissive—traits that are not naturally exclusive to men or women, but that vary with culture, class, ethnicity, and other social statuses.

Views of *women as property* are prevalent globally. In Western societies, rape was originally seen as a property crime against the father or husband of the victim, resulting in diminished value of the

Myths/Attitudes About Violence Against Women

Myth	Rape
"Women enjoy it; women want it."	It wasn't rape, only rough sex; women say no when they mean yes.
"Women ask for it."	Women provoke rape by dressing attractively, leading men on, and going out alone.
"It happens only to certain types of women."	Rape happens only to poor women, women from certain areas, and so on.
"Women lie or make false accusations."	Women falsely accuse men for revenge or to protect their reputations.
"Men are justified, not responsible."	He paid for the date; he had to release his sexual tension; he thought she wanted it.
"It's not really harmful."	She wasn't a virgin; there are no bruises.
"These acts are very unusual or deviant."	He was drinking and not himself; he must be sick or under stress.

Adapted from Mary Koss et al.'s 1994 book *No Safe Haven: Male Violence Against Women at Home, at Work, and in the Community*; original chart adapted from Louise F. Fitzgerald's *The Last Great Open Secret: The Sexual Harassment of Women in the Workplace and Academia*, 1993; and Liz Kelly's *Surviving Sexual Violence*, 1988.

Battering	Sexual Harassment
Women don't leave, so they must like being battered.	Women invite and feel flattered by sexual attention.
Women provoke men: nagging them, arguing with them, and so forth.	Women flirt.
Battering happens to bad housewives, poor women, women of color, or women who saw violence as children.	Women who think they've been harassed are just being paranoid, or they have an ax to grind.
It wasn't violence, only a fight.	The accusers are disgruntled workers.
He had a bad day at work; it was punishment for unwifely behavior; he didn't mean it; she knows how to upset him.	He's just trying to be nice to her; he's expressing an interest in her.
She didn't break any bones; she'll heal.	He didn't hurt her; she didn't lose her job or her promotion.
He was drinking and not himself; he must be sick or under stress and needs help and understanding.	He was drinking and not himself; he's under a lot of stress and needs help.

woman ("damaged goods"). This view of women as property has been established historically as being at the root of social attitudes about rape and domestic violence. It can be found in Western laws, customs, and religious beliefs. Early marriage laws gave men the legal right to hit their wives. Laws in the United States were modeled after English common law, which expected men to be responsible for and physically "discipline" wives, who had no legal status separate from husbands or fathers and, after marriage, were owned and controlled by their husbands. Early British rape law similarly required that restitution for rape be paid to the victim's husband or, if the victim was not married, to her father. While early U.S. criminal laws against rape and domestic violence did not completely conform to British common law, and were reformed during the 1980s, remnants of the early laws persist in attitudes and actual practices within justice systems.

Twenty years ago, researcher Murray Straus called the marriage license a "hitting license," and some violence researchers believe the husband's ownership and control of the wife is embedded in the marriage contract. This ownership extends to dating and other intimate relationships and continues after a marriage ends. Men's entitlement to women's bodies and exclusive attention, and to intrude upon women's physical space without thought, stem from these assumptions and attitudes, even though women's rights to be autonomous from men have gradually changed during the past century.

Pervasive beliefs that women are responsible for men's emotional and sexual well-being, without regard to any harmful consequences for women, are often openly stated by men when they justify rape and abuse. Abusers often express their "right" to take out their frustrations, insecurities, and anger on certain women, such as their wives or girlfriends, or to punish them for not being exclusively available whenever they want or need them. They do not target others at random; they target those they feel entitled to control.

Rape culture refers to a set of values and beliefs that create an environment conducive to rape, based on assumptions that men are aggressive and women are passive and acquiescent. These assumptions about gender contain a double standard in which men who are sexually aggressive are viewed positively as manly and successful, whereas women who enjoy sex or engage in premarital sex are seen as "sluts" and demeaned. These attitudes are the basis for myths about rape such as "She wanted it," "Girls say no when they mean yes," or "Women lead men on."

Male bonding in peer groups contributes to a dynamic seen in hypermasculine settings, such as the military, athletics, gangs, and fraternities, in which men bond in brotherhood, and prove their masculinity to one another, by objectifying or sexually coercing or assaulting women. In these circumstances, men who might not rape individually do so in a group that pressures men to fit the distorted and stereotyped ideal of the sexually aggressive, masculine man. The group attacks a woman who represents the faceless "other," the object of their fear and hatred that men must avoid resembling at all costs— the distorted feminine stereotype of a woman.

Carole Sheffield writes, in her essay "Sexual Terrorism," that "the right to control the female body is the cornerstone of patriarchy." *Patriarchy* is a system of social structures and practices, in which men dominate, oppress, and exploit women. Whether we conceptualize this social phenomenon as patriarchy or as *male supremacy* or *male domination*, feminists view it as a consistent pattern of ideological

Who Should Be Restricted?

Israeli Prime Minister Golda Meir met with her cabinet to discuss a series of rapes that had occurred in the state. Her all-male cabinet suggested addressing the problem by instituting a 9:00 PM curfew for women and girls; after a lengthy discussion, Meir said that since the rapists were men, a better solution would be to institute a curfew for men instead. According to Meir, the cabinet was silent for a time—and then decided against a curfew.

and structural practices that serve to justify and perpetuate men's oppression of women. Susan Brownmiller, in her groundbreaking 1975 book *Against Our Will: Men, Women and Rape,* wrote that rape is the "enforcer of male supremacy, the use of the penis as weapon" and "the conscious process of intimidation by which all men keep all women in a state of fear."

Sheffield defines sexual terrorism as the system by which men frighten women to control and dominate them, a system with the same characteristics as other forms of terrorism. This includes nonviolent sexual intimidation and the threat of violence as well as overt sexual violence. Its institutionalization is reflected in laws, in rape during war, and in slavery worldwide. As Lisa Price writes in *Feminist Frameworks: Building Theory on Violence Against Women,* her excellent analysis of feminist theory on violence against women, "Experience with political terrorism has shown that its strength lies largely in its unpredictability, targeting a whole population but selecting individual victims randomly." Unlike other crimes, crimes of violence against females cut across socioeconomic lines. These are the crimes least likely to be reported, and when reported, they are the crimes least likely to be brought to trial or to result in conviction. They are often blamed on the victim; they are generally not taken seriously; and they fuse dominance and sexuality. As British researcher Elizabeth Stanko wrote, "All women have some experience of male violation. . . . *To walk the streets warily at night is how we actually feel our femininity."*

In their daily work, lawyers, advocates, and counselors who see men and/or boys charged with acquaintance rape, intimate partner violence, or other violence against women observe perpetrators' shock and disbelief that anyone thinks they have done something illegal or wrong. Rapists are often genuinely surprised to learn that the victim has called the police or is seriously injured, thinking, "She wanted it!" One young man told a police officer when he was arrested for assault and battery, "What do you mean this is illegal?! She's my girlfriend!"

Any female can be a victim. The perpetrators—child molesters, batterers, wife beaters, rapists—often do not understand they have

Defendants' Rights

The justice system guarantees defendants certain rights that are fundamental to democracy, such as due process, innocence until guilt is proven beyond doubt, and freedom from incarceration once perpetrators have completed their sentences. Justice systems in the United States are challenged by activists because so few cases of violence against women are prosecuted, and so few result in prison sentences. Men who are imprisoned are predominantly men of color, even though statistics indicate that white men perpetrate more violence than Hispanic and black men. Some women of color who are imprisoned have been forced to participate in the criminal behavior of men who have abused them. There are many reasons for these injustices—the foremost being pervasive prejudicial attitudes stereotyping people of color and blaming women for their victimization. Very often when crimes such as rape, domestic violence, and forced prostitution are committed, there are no witnesses (other than the victim), so trials focus on what is commonly referred to as a "he said, she said" situation—and the victim is likely not to be believed because of these attitudes.

Protecting defendants' rights is necessary and important but may contribute to complaints about perpetrators "getting away with" their crimes. In criminal trials, defendants' rights are clear, but the victim's role is as a witness, without the same rights. Therefore victims' testimony is given in a setting in which women's stories are discredited, especially those of women of color. For example, defense attorneys' primary strategy for defending men charged with rape is to discredit women's accounts, claim that they lied about consenting to sex, and humiliate them in court and the media.

done anything wrong, views that are often shared by judges, police, and others. Sexual violence is rarely punished; an estimated 5 percent of reported rape cases result in convictions. Several studies of complaints by women abused by intimate partners found that none had resulted in convictions.

There are many ways that the fear of violence affects women: for example, how we dress, where and when we go out, where we work, and the kinds of work and other activities we do. Think about the ways we judge women who have been raped. Women are often asked what they did to bring it upon themselves, how they dressed, what they were doing that provoked it, and so on. Class makes a difference in the degree of choice women have about where they go, what hours they work, how vulnerable they are to rape. Therefore, violence against women functions as a means of social control in the same way that justifying and threatening violence enforces oppression against any group.

Culture, Religion, and Violence

Cultural values and beliefs play a significant role in shaping a woman's experience of violence and abuse and its meaning to her. While domestic violence, rape, sexual harassment, trafficking of women, and other forms of violence take place in every part of the world, several forms of abuse take place primarily in certain regions or cultures, such as honor killings and female genital cutting. Individual, family, and community responses to all of them vary significantly among cultural, religious, and ethnic groups. A woman's real and perceived options for addressing violence differ based on her sense of self as a member of a family and community.

An important aspect of culture is its view of the value of individualism or collectivism—in other words, values about the relative priority of one's own goals and desires and those of the collective to which one belongs. For example, Western and U.S. cultures are generally individualist; Asian cultures are generally collectivist. In general, collectivist cultures emphasize obedience to and harmony within the group while individualist cultures emphasize personal satisfaction, achievement, and autonomy. Another and related cultural value is the relative looseness or tightness of a culture and the level of tolerance for diverse, nonconforming behavior. Individualist cultures tend to be looser, as there is more acceptance of individual choice. For women in loose individualist cultures, a range of work and lifestyle options are available. In contrast, tight collectivist cultures are characterized by specific norms that regulate social interaction and have strong negative social consequences (i.e., shame, loss of face) for those who deviate from the prescribed role behavior. The goal of the tight collectivist family structure is to control the individual to protect and preserve the group. A result is that it leads to invisibility of the individual, and especially of women, in collectivist cultures where women's roles are restricted as bearers of children and teachers of cultural norms.

There are cultural as well as psychological and economic contexts underlying decisions made by women who have experienced violence and abuse. Deciding to report rape or to leave a battering husband may lead to rejection by a religious community that opposes divorce or sees women as responsible for rape. It may lead to the loss of ties to a woman's extended family and community if they believe the woman's actions to be shameful to them.

Study reports and other writings about violence against women often describe cultural obstructions to women's safety from men's violence— for example, Asian cultural expectations of women's subservience to men, or Hispanic cultural valuing of women's silent endurance of suffering. However, there is less recognition of the ways that cultures also empower and support women. Community ties and cultural and religious values are sources of strength for many people. When in a crisis, people are likely to call on their faith or community for strength, moral support, or assistance. Modern cultures are complex, too, and have many variations from one family or community to another. We must not summarize a culture's view of violence against women in only one dimension. Every culture has beliefs that disenfranchise women as well as beliefs that empower them.

Cultural beliefs also interact with other beliefs on the part of individuals and families dealing with male violence. Studies of domestic violence indicate that both male batterers and battered women tend to have more rigid stereotyped or "traditional" (for their cultures) gender role expectations than people not in abusive relationships.

Cultural explanations are often used to describe social influences on the use of violence against women by men from ethnic minority groups in the United States, whereas psychological explanations (e.g., "Perpetrators are mentally ill, stressed, or short-tempered") are more often used for Western European Americans. Americans seem to overlook Western culture as a factor influencing behavior, unaware of the tendency to view what is American as "normal" and to perceive "culture" as somehow non-American, an influential factor for people who are seen as "other," "not like us."

Even though Americans tend to see violence against women as a problem experienced by other cultures, the United States as a nation seems to have a greater tolerance for and incidence of violence than other postindustrial countries. Historian Eric Monkkonen found convincing proof that violence has been endemic to American culture for more than two centuries. He told a *Los Angeles Times* reporter that "the U.S. has tolerated a homicide rate much higher than all of the rest of the Western world except Russia." He found that murder is a crime committed mostly by men in the heat of passion "to assert manliness, power or territory." There are many examples of our cultural tendency to justify the use of violence to solve problems and conflicts and to glorify and make heroes of those who do so: gratuitous violence in the media, high rates of individual gun ownership, community violence and violent crime rates, aggression in sports, and violent images in computer games are among the many examples.

Cultural and religious beliefs about dating, marriage, divorce, sexuality, and gender roles influence the ways survivors and victims of violence understand or explain why they have been victimized, how they judge themselves and/or others, and the decisions they make about protecting themselves, telling others, or extricating themselves from violence and abuse. Attitudes about seeking help outside the family influence victims' access to and use of resources and supports.

Najma's story (see sidebar) is an example of the use of the "cultural defense" in legal settings. It is the acceptance of cultural explanations for individual behavior and of certain women as legitimate victims. Judges and others congratulate themselves on being culturally sensitive when they view violence as normal to a culture, but they demean the

Najma's Story

After heart-wrenching deliberations, Najma Sultana, a Pakistani woman in New Jersey, decided to seek a temporary restraining order against her abusive husband. This was not an easy decision for her. She was going against her family, which urged her to be patient; her religion, which affirmed that virtuous women are always tolerant; her two children, who were crying for their father; her community, which sneered at women who invited outside interference into the family; and everything she had learned about marriage, love, and women's role in society. She was also working against her fear of being alone with meager resources in a foreign country. In retaliation, Najma's husband, much more conversant in the ways of this country, secured a restraining order against her. A few days later, when both appeared before the family court judge, there were no doubts that Najma was a battered woman and that her husband's claims were baseless. Yet the judge, who vacated both of their restraining orders, stated that such treatment of wives may be an accepted practice in the couple's native culture and that, therefore, the husband has probably acted in accordance with his cultural beliefs.

Excerpted from Shamita Das Dasgupta's "Women's Realities: Defining Violence Against Women by Immigration, Race, and Class," in Raquel Kennedy Bergen's *Issues in Intimate Violence*.

perpetrator and the culture, and they neglect their responsibility to hold all people equally accountable for the consequences of their use of violence. Use of culture in this way facilitates the decriminalization of violence against women, and it can be dangerous to women.

The Christian tradition has perpetuated the tendency to blame the victim of sexual violence. According to the Reverend Marie Fortune, founder of the FaithTrust Institute in Seattle, "The dualistic view of the mind-body split assigned the sexual or carnal self to women and provided justification for women's subordination." She explains, "[The] view of women as 'the devil's gateway' was only one example," adding that the Protestant reformers Martin Luther and John Calvin both

34 WOMEN AND VIOLENCE

made allowances for wife beating (unless it threatened a woman's life).
Some church leaders, such as Luther, were unapologetic about their
own physical violence toward their wives. Likewise within Judaism and
within Islam, we find selected texts and teachings that are used to justify
abuse of women, although the original texts also note that wife beating
was not to be tolerated. The Shulchan Aruch, the legal code of Judaism,
is clear that a man cannot force his wife to engage in sexual relations,
nor is he permitted to abuse his wife in any way. Muhammad, in his
last sermon, said that men should "treat your women well, and be kind
to them, for they are your partners and committed helpers."

Marie Fortune concludes, "Sexual and domestic violence must be
understood theologically and ethically as sin, that is, as the physical,
psychological, and spiritual violation of a person by another person;
as such, it violates the bodily integrity of the victim and shatters any
possibility of right relationship between the victim and abuser."

Racism and Discrimination

Women who have experienced racism and discrimination against
themselves or others in their communities may feel conflicted loyalty
when considering their need for protection from violence. African
American and Hispanic women may sympathize with what men suffer
in their daily lives and in the criminal justice system because they are
more likely to be arrested, prosecuted, and jailed than white men. Asian
women may be reluctant to report violence or seek help, wanting to
keep from bringing shame to their families. Based on their experiences,
Native American women may not expect law enforcement agencies to
investigate rape by non-Native American men. Women of color may
not trust that they will be protected or treated seriously by systems
such as hospitals, law enforcement, mental health providers, or social
services. They often fear excessive interference and scrutiny from public
agencies, especially mothers who fear having their children taken from
them. Based on her research, scholar and activist Beth Richie reports in
Natalie Sokoloff's anthology *Domestic Violence at the Margins: Readings
on Race, Class, Gender, and Culture* that women of color "who turn to

Violence Against Native Women

Native American and Alaska Native tribal law specialist Sarah Deer is a citizen of the Muscogee (Creek) Nation and the coeditor of the anthology *Sharing Our Stories of Survival: Native Women Surviving Violence*. The following statement is assembled from her answers, on the Amnesty International website, to questions submitted by Amnesty supporters regarding Native women and violence:

> *Many Native women I have talked to have suggested that the USA was, in a sense, "founded" upon the rape of women. The Europeans who came here felt entitled to take the land and the women. Women were considered property by many of the Europeans who came to this continent. There is still much work to be done to address this mentality. Sexual predators know that rape of Native women is an under-reported and under-prosecuted crime. The Department of Justice statistics consistently indicate that the vast majority of sexual predators against Native women are non-Native. This is an anomaly in criminology. No one knows for sure why this is, but some experts theorize it has to do with jurisdictional authority. Tribal nations cannot prosecute non-Indian offenders, so there may be a connection.*

the police for protection still face wrongful arrest, degradation from officers, and deportation in the case of immigrant families. Overall, the state disproportionately arrests and oppresses men of color. Research indicates that in some communities women of color are initially reluctant to call the police and are significantly deterred from making a second call for help given the impact of incarceration on men in their neighborhoods. Intimate partner violence as a law and order problem has backfired for women of color."

Immigrant women are especially vulnerable to sexual and domestic violence. In a 2004 *New York Times* piece, reporters Nina Bernstein and Leslie Kaufman cite a New York City Health Department study finding that "lovers and husbands were responsible for almost 60 percent of the deaths of women between 20 and 50 . . . and such victims were 87 percent more likely than those killed by strangers to be foreign-born. . . . Just over 50 percent of all the women killed by intimate partners were immigrants." Immigrant women are vulnerable to intimate partner violence, sexual violence, and sexual exploitation. Because of language barriers, isolation, and lack of access to organizations to assist them, they often lack information they need—for example, they may not know their legal rights or be aware of the resources available to them. They are often afraid of "making trouble" that might lead to deportation, especially if their residency status is not legal. They may lack support systems or financial resources and so have limited options for freedom from violence. They face obstacles related to attitudes toward immigrants, especially non-European immigrants, in the United States.

Shamita Dasgupta is a law professor at New York University and founder of Manavi Inc., an organization that focuses on violence against women in the South Asian community. She argues that immigration may be a mixed experience for some women: it may help them escape limitations imposed by oppressive social structures of extended families in their countries of origin, but it may also deprive them of the protections their families and communities provide. For example, in South Asia, a man's abusive behavior may, to some extent, be monitored by other family members, neighbors, and in-laws. "Community shame can also be evoked to restrain an abuser," Dasgupta explains. "[Thus,] being in a country where a strong sense of family and community is absent may actually pressure immigrant women to cling more tenaciously to their nuclear families."

The Intersectionality of Race, Class, and Gender

Kimberlé Crenshaw, a law professor and leader in the intellectual movement called critical race theory, introduced the term "intersectionality," a theory that explains the realities of women who simultaneously experience diverse oppressions, including but not limited to gender violence (violence against women because they are female). Crenshaw defines it as "a conceptualization of the problem that attempts to capture both the structural and dynamic consequences of the interaction between two or more axes of subordination." Feminist writer bell hooks refers to this intersection as "interlocking systems of domination which uphold and sustain one another." Race, class, and gender, she explains, are not completely separate issues or identities but intersect and interact with one another in a way that makes the experience of violence qualitatively different. Some women are targets of violence because of their gender *and* their race *and* their ethnicity *and* their socioeconomic status. And the intersectionality of sexual orientation with other identities related to class, gender, and ethnicity makes same-sex partner violence a multilayered phenomenon, distinctly different from abuse in heterosexual relationships.

Longtime activist and author Angela Davis and others address the impact of the history of rape in African American women's lives. Sexual coercion was an essential dimension of the social relations between slave master and slaves, and of the property rights that structured those relations. "While there has been a great deal written about the motivation of black men to rape the women of their oppressors," Davis writes, "there is no psychosexual history of slavery that explores the meaning of white male sexual exploitation of black women or the politics of sexuality—rape by the master of slave women, and sexual humiliation of white wives in the process." White men who wanted to marry black slave women they loved were labeled insane.

This history has been replaced by the colonization story invented by white men about the overwhelming, desperate longing that black men have to sexually violate the bodies of white women. As bell hooks has written, this is a story of revenge against domination by white men, and of rape as a weapon by which dominated and oppressed black men regain power over white men. This story has led to lynching of black men.

Social theorist Patricia Hill Collins explains that "at the heart of both racism and sexism are notions of biological determinism claiming that people of African descent and women possess immutable biological characteristics marking their inferiority to elite white men." Crenshaw adds, "When black women were raped by white males, they were being raped not as women generally, but as black women specifically. Their femaleness made them sexually vulnerable to racist domination, while their blackness effectively denied them any protection."

Women's Rights Are Human Rights

There are two levels of human rights: individual rights and structural rights. Individual rights comprise individual socioeconomic, political, and sexual rights: rights to life, safety from violence, employment without discrimination, due process, and basic needs such as food, water, housing, and education. Structural rights address the economic, gender, and ethnic inequalities underlying socioeconomic and political structures that affect individual rights: the human right to freedom from torture, women's right to fair representation in government, and the right to equality between women and men in all spheres. Human rights are universal; women everywhere are entitled to the same rights as men, and all human rights are equally important.

The human rights perspective recognizes the importance of economic, social, cultural, civil, and political rights, and it holds governments, not just individual perpetrators, responsible for the violation of women's rights to life, liberty, and security of person; to physical and mental health; to freedom from torture; and to effective remedy (access to justice).

Activists in the United States are just beginning to develop strategies for addressing violence against women as a violation of human rights. In an innovative effort to advocate for reform of family courts, the Battered Mothers' Testimony Project applied a human rights analysis to battered mothers' experiences in the Massachusetts family court system. It identified six intersecting categories of human rights violations there: The courts, the project found, had failed to protect battered women and children from abuse; showed discrimination and bias against battered women; treated battered women degradingly; denied due process to battered women; allowed the batterer to continue his abuse through the family courts; and failed to respect the economic human rights of battered women and children. Its 2002 report, *Battered Mothers Speak*

A Perspective of Race

The following excerpt is from bell hooks's *Yearning: Race, Gender, and Cultural Politics.*

A black woman friend called to say that she had been attacked on the street by a black man. He took her purse, her house keys, her car keys. She lives in one of the poorest cities in the U.S. We talked about poverty, sexism and racial domination to place what had happened in a perspective that will enable both individual healing and political understanding of this crime. Today I heard this story. A white woman friend called to say that she had been attacked in her doorway by a black man. She screamed and he ran away. Neighbors coming to her aid invoked racism. She refused to engage in this discussion even though she was shocked by the intensity and degree of racism expressed. Even in the midst of her own fear and pain, she remained politically aware, so as not to be complicit in perpetuating the white supremacy that is the root of so much suffering. Both of these women feel rage at their victimizers; they do not absolve them even as they seek to understand and to respond in ways that will enrich the struggle to end domination—so that sexism, sexist violence, racism and racist violence will cease to be an everyday happening.

Out, emphasized the government's responsibility for violating battered women's rights as the focus for reform and change.

Violence against women is a human rights issue. When the state dismisses the majority of violence against women as a private or domestic problem, this violence is condoned. It is justified as being a part of culture and tradition, which serves only to justify the systematic denial of rights that is rooted in unequal power relationships.

Discrimination and violence against women result from the structural relationships of power, domination, and privilege that men have in relation to women in society. Gender-based violence is a form of discrimination against women, and the human rights and women's rights movements challenge governments to take responsibility for eliminating it.

"Marcha contra el femicidio." A woman and child attend a march to protest femicide on February 29, 2008, in Viña del Mar, Chile. In 2007, there were sixty-two femicides in Chile. In 2008, as of this publication, there were twenty. For this reason, protests have been mounted across the country, particularly in Santiago, the capital. © Fernanda Trivelli

CHAPTER 2

GLOBAL PERSPECTIVES

ACCORDING TO THE WOMEN'S FUNDING NETWORK in 2007, seven out of ten of the world's hungry are women and girls, the majority of whom are illiterate with no access to basic amenities such as safe drinking water. Two-thirds of the 130 million children worldwide who are not in school are girls. Between 75 percent and 80 percent of the world's twenty-seven million refugees are women and children. Women hold 17.3 percent of the seats in the world's parliaments. The majority of women earn, on average, about three-fourths of the pay of males for the same work. More than two-thirds of the world's unpaid work is done by women. One in every four households in the world is now headed by a woman. The primary victims of today's armed conflicts are civilian women and children, not soldiers, with rape becoming more evident as a weapon of war. Women are extremely vulnerable to exploitation and violence.

Our newspapers and Internet are filled with dramatic stories of injustices in women's lives all over the world. Women are raped in Sudan's Darfur region, women are trafficked from Guatemala for prostitution in Los Angeles, apologies have been sought from Japan for the kidnapping and sexual enslavement of World War II Korean "comfort women," and women are raped and tortured in Myanmar: these are examples from recent newspaper headlines. We know more than ever before about events and people in places that until fairly recently we would not have heard about. Growth and development in technology, communications, tourism, international aid and activism, and the global economy have expanded our access to information and our impact on people and places far from the United States. We can read blogs written by Iraqi women, study reports from African women's conferences on peace and nonviolence, or look up statistics on the occurrence of domestic violence in the United Kingdom. We have learned that violence against women is widespread in every nation and community, with many patterns similar to those in the United States, and also with great differences from one region to the next.

The United Nations estimates that one in three women globally experience some form of victimization in childhood, adolescence, or adulthood. In 2002, the World Health Organization (WHO) gathered data from hundreds of surveys and research reports, as well as from statistics submitted by national governments, and concluded that "although differing methodologies make country-to-country comparisons tricky, the totality shows that women and children bear a disproportionate burden of sexual violence and violence by family members or intimates." Another WHO study in 2005 on women's health and domestic violence surveyed twenty-four thousand women ages fifteen to forty-nine in fifteen sites in ten countries (Bangladesh, Brazil, Ethiopia, Japan, Peru, Namibia, Samoa, Serbia and Montenegro, Thailand, and Tanzania). Between one-third and three-quarters (35 percent to 76 percent) of the women had been sexually or physically assaulted by someone since they were fifteen, the majority by a former or current partner.

Other studies show that in the Australian state of Victoria, violence by intimate partners results in more ill health and premature death among women of reproductive age than any other risk factor, including high blood pressure, obesity, and smoking. Intimate partner violence accounts for 40 percent to 60 percent of female homicides in many countries, and an important portion of maternal mortality in India, Bangladesh, and the United States (compared with about 5 percent of men killed by current or former partners).

The 2005 WHO study also found that at least one-fifth (21 percent to 66 percent) of women reporting physical violence in the study had never told anyone of their partner's violence before the study interview. In one of the most important findings of the study, the authors reported that

> *in about half of the sites, 50 to 90 percent of women agreed that it is acceptable for a man to beat his wife under one or more of the following circumstances: if she disobeys her husband, refuses him sex, does not complete the housework on time, asks about other women, is unfaithful, or is suspected of infidelity. This was higher among women who had experienced abuse than among those who had not, and may indicate either that women experiencing violence learn to "accept" or rationalize this abuse, or that women are at greater risk of violence in communities where a substantial proportion of individuals condone abuse.*

As Sarah Henderson and Alana Jeydel point out in their book, *Participation and Protest: Women and Politics in a Global World*, there are issues that are universal to women all over the world: access to education, stable employment, adequate political representation, and physical and mental well-being. However, achieving these goals is a different process for women in the developing world than it is for Western women. For example, they say, a woman in Africa faces a one in sixteen chance of dying in childbirth, while a woman in a developed country faces a one in twenty-eight hundred risk. They highlight women's lack of power in the household, lack of government funding for healthcare, and endemic poverty as the main reasons for this extreme disparity.

Economic globalization has resulted in improved resources for some women, but it has also exacerbated conditions that worsen other women's vulnerability to exploitation and violence.

Globalization's Effects on Women

Women have become more vulnerable, and violence against them has become more prevalent, under economic systems in which governments' strategic approach to poverty is to open up the land and labor to multinational corporations at the expense of national sovereignty and people's rights to food, land, and resources. Promoting privatization and the growth of multinational corporations under the guise of creating jobs and boosting economies, governments and corporations have increased the wealth of only a small sector of their economies, the wealthiest, while destroying access to independent means of economic survival, safety, and security for large numbers of people. The liberalization of trade among nations based on agreements such as the North American Free Trade Agreement (NAFTA)—and the efforts of international economic organizations such as the World Trade Organization (WTO) to increase growth of large industries in debt-ridden countries—has had complex effects on many working people worldwide. Established in 1994, NAFTA lifted most tariffs on goods traded among the United States, Mexico, and Canada, aiming to facilitate cross-border movement of goods and services and substantially increase investment. Its core provisions grant foreign investors a remarkable set of new rights and privileges that have promoted relocation abroad of factories and jobs, and the privatization and deregulation of essential services, such as water, energy, and healthcare.

The WTO, established in 1995, is an international organization that deals with the rules of trade between nations. It is a multilateral trading system for administering trade agreements, facilitating trade negotiations, and resolving trade disputes. It provides training and technical assistance for developing countries. The WTO is one of the main mechanisms of corporate globalization. Critics worldwide see it as primarily functioning to open markets for the benefit of transnational corporations at the expense of national and local economies; workers, farmers, indigenous peoples, women, and other social groups; health and safety; the environment; and animal welfare.

According to Anuradha Mittal, codirector of Food First/The Institute for Food Development Policy, one example of how the organization functions is the WTO Agreement on Agriculture, which requires that countries open their economies and import agricultural products from other countries. American markets are saturated, so the United States is aggressively—and successfully—pressuring foreign markets to import U.S. products. One out of three U.S. acres produces food or fiber for export. The United States subsidizes agriculture, which benefits agribusiness, but these subsidies are denied to poor farmers, and they lower world prices. For example, the United States exports wheat at 46 percent and corn at 20 percent below cost of production; family farmers in the United States, and in countries with which the United States trades, can't afford to sell their produce below cost. So, as Mittal explains, the WTO agreement puts control of the food system in the hands of large businesses, export producers, and the wealthy few (such as investors).

Before NAFTA, Mexico used restrictive licensing and high tariffs to control its grain imports. Now, though, the United States and Canada pay no tariffs for grain exports to Mexico. Economist Debbie Seidband reported in 2004 that Mexico, once self-sufficient in producing basic food needs, now imports 95 percent of its soy, 58 percent of its rice, 49 percent of its wheat, and 40 percent of its meat. Mexico's demand for U.S. corn reached record highs in 2004. As a result, Mexican corn farmers are being put out of business. Two million of Mexico's extreme poor are corn farmers; they can't compete with subsidized American agribusiness. Mittal estimates that six hundred peasant farmers are forced off their land every day. This is happening in many other countries as well.

Although some see the movement of labor from small farms to wage-earning factory jobs as improving a nation's standard of living, these efforts have led to the economic and cultural dislocation of rural and indigenous people in regions of South and Central America and the Asia Pacific countries. The growth of large-scale industries, such as mining, logging, power generation, and agriculture, operated

The Women of Juárez

Since 1993, more than 370 women have been murdered, and about seventy others have disappeared, in Mexico's Ciudad Juárez. In many of the cases, victims were discovered in an open area, lying between piles of rubbish, half naked, with their hands tied behind their backs. Forensic reports indicate that many of the murdered women were sexually assaulted and tortured before death.

In a dramatic example of the link between globalization and violence against women, many of the murder victims had migrated for economic reasons from other areas of Mexico to Ciudad Juárez, where they lived in marginalized communities, often with no support structure. Many were employed in maquiladoras, non-Mexican-owned assembly plants, across the border from El Paso, Texas, that produce finished goods for the United States.

Since the passage of NAFTA, Mexico has allowed materials used in maquiladoras to enter the country duty-free, provided the finished product is then immediately exported out of Mexico. Companies have been drawn to Ciudad Juárez by these tax advantages, by the ease of exporting to the United States, and by the area's cheap labor (about $.50 to $1.50/hour). About three hundred such plants are situated on the city's outskirts.

In some maquiladoras, women are recruited for jobs based on their attractive appearance and instructed to wear makeup. The average age of women workers is seventeen, and they are required to work from early morning until late at night. They are often sexually harassed by male bosses and coworkers. Although forced by poverty to migrate to support their

by multinational corporations, has caused poverty, loss of land and traditional sources of livelihood, and inconsistent access to food. Multinational companies forming agribusiness ventures have turned subsistence farmers from landowners to cheap laborers who have no control over pricing, land use, or distribution of produce.

To survive poverty and to support their families, hundreds of thousands of men and women have joined the pool of cheap labor; many have migrated to cities where they can earn wages. Women and children are the worst affected. Migration of men to cities often families, they have often been portrayed by local police officials and the media as "loose" women, or whores living away from their homes and families, because by being single, leaving home, and working in factories they are not conforming to traditional norms for women.

It isn't known who is committing the Juárez murders—some attribute the killings to powerful drug cartels operating in the area, while others blame serial killers or domestic violence—but what does seem evident, as Max Blumenthal writes in his award-winning 2002 *Salon* article "Day of the Dead," is this:

> *The murders arise from a social landscape that has been transformed by global economic forces. Where Ciudad Juarez was once a small, sleepy desert outpost just across the border from El Paso, Texas, the population in the past decade has exploded to 1.2 million people, many of them drawn by the lure of the maquiladoras. The tides of people have overwhelmed the ability of the city to absorb them, overwhelmed health services, social services and law enforcement. Free-trade advocates once promised that NAFTA would transform Juarez into the City of the Future—and they have been proven right in a way they never could have imagined.*

The murders have been committed with impunity because there has been little official effort to investigate and solve them, enabling the perpetrators to avoid legal action, apparently with collusion from the local police and government officials. Owners of the maquiladoras and the U.S. companies that do business with them have ignored the situation.

leaves women to fend for themselves as well as for their households and their communities. Migration of women and girls to cities leaves them poor and far from their communities and families, where they are more vulnerable than ever to sexual harassment, sexual assault, trafficking, and sexual slavery. Since NAFTA was signed in 1994, more than twenty-seven hundred sweatshops producing goods for export (called maquiladoras) have begun operations in Mexico; they employ more than 1.3 million workers, mostly young women. Women's pay averages 50 cents an hour, without job security or benefits, and they are often subject to unsafe working conditions and sexual harassment. These women live in a harsh environment that often denies them access to effective protection from the criminal justice system.

According to Radhika Coomaraswamy, the UN Special Rapporteur on Violence Against Women, in Hong Kong alone there were 237,110 foreign domestic helpers in 2002, the majority coming from the Philippines, Indonesia, and Thailand, all women. In Southeast Asia, women and girls are being trafficked for the sex industry as well as for sweatshop labor, forced marriage, and street begging. Coomaraswamy has said that the problem of trafficking in women and girls has increased in recent years as part of the "feminine side" of globalization.

Private market interests are reducing the role of governments, and subcontracting of manufacturing by large corporations has led to deregulation, an absence of laws to protect workers, and the increase of "sweatshop" labor in jobs that offer no fixed incomes or benefits. While globalization has created economic opportunities for women in some areas, increased poverty and loss of sources of income have led thousands of women to migrate to factory towns in search of work, which often makes them vulnerable to abuse, exploitation, and violence.

Human Trafficking

The Coalition to Abolish Slavery and Trafficking (CAST) defines human trafficking as the recruitment and transportation of persons within or across national boundaries by force, fraud, or deception, for the purpose of exploiting them economically. Trafficked people most commonly work in sweatshops, restaurants, on farms, in manufacturing, in prostitution, and in private homes as domestic workers. They are subjected to a condition of slavery through deception, confiscation of their identity documents, forced labor (work without pay), physical, psychological, and sexual violence (or the threat of it), and debt bondage. "Debt bondage" refers to being forced to work off the costs of room and board, as well as the costs of transportation to the recipient country, instead of being paid wages for work.

Trafficking routes change in response to economic and political changes. In general, developed or developing countries are receiving countries, while sending countries are the poorest countries with the lowest level of development or countries going through major disruptions such as economic crises, natural disasters, or civil wars. Human trafficking is a multibillion-dollar industry, similar to drug trafficking, generating an estimated $5 billion to $6 billion in gross earnings per year. Most commonly conducted by gangs or organized crime groups, trafficking succeeds because of the overt or covert collusion or corruption of government officials.

Trafficked women are often treated as illegal immigrants by the governments of receiving countries when they attempt to flee from those who enslave them, which deprives them of needed help and makes them vulnerable to revictimization.

Sex Trafficking

It is mainly women and children who are forced into services of sexual exploitation by means of violence, dominance, debt bondage, deception, or other forms of coercion. There is evidence that every year

Juana's Story

Mr. A brought Juana to the United States from one of his business trips to Colombia to work in his family's household, cleaning and taking care of the children. Once she arrived, he and his wife never let Juana leave the house on her own, and they kept her in slavelike conditions. One day, after two years, she left the house when no one was there, and she kept walking until she saw someone she thought would help her. Law enforcement authorities listened to her story and investigated and arrested Mr. A. However, as an undocumented immigrant, Juana was detained for deportation. Because Mr. A had repeatedly threatened to harm her family in Colombia, she feared that he would find her again.

hundreds of thousands of women are trafficked and exploited within the transnational prostitution industry. The conditions under which they are often forced to live lead to multiple serious health problems as well as violence and abuse.

Like any other commercial market, the trade in women and girls is driven by the economic dynamics of supply and demand. David Batstone, in his book *Not for Sale: The Return of the Global Slave Trade—And How We Can Fight It*, explains the interaction between poverty and social inequality and traffickers' easy access to large numbers of girls. Desperately poor parents may sell their children or at least be susceptible to scams that will allow the trafficker to take control over their children's lives. Young women in vulnerable communities are more likely to take a risk on a job offer in a faraway location. Poor people are apt to accept loans from traffickers who can later manipulate and entrap them. "All of these paths carry unsuspecting recruits into the supply chains of slavery," Batstone writes.

In most instances, developed or developing countries with well-established sex industries are receiving countries (Japan, Germany, the United States, the Netherlands, Thailand, Taiwan, Korea, and India). Poorer countries with the lowest level of development or in the midst of civil war are more likely to send women and children abroad. Historically, there is a pattern of outmigration from poorer to wealthier countries.

Sex trafficking has been best documented in Asia. Southeast Asia sustains a major sex trafficking industry, possibly the worst in the world; it is a large exporter of women and girls for forced prostitution in the United States, Europe, Japan, China, and Australia. The economic and social forces of change that feed the sex trade are at work in Southeast Asia: Cambodia, Thailand, Vietnam, Laos, and Myanmar—both receiving and sending countries—have had devastating poverty, rapid industrialization, exploding population growth, and armed conflicts. Poverty forces families to send their daughters to work in uncertain circumstances, increasing their vulnerability to being trafficked and forced into sex work, or forcing them to choose to work as prostitutes.

Rapid industrialization requires a workforce shift from family-based businesses or farms to factories generally located in or near cities where there are enough workers; this shift disrupts families and their ability to protect their children, increasing women and girls' vulnerability to exploitation. Population growth and armed conflict also cause major social and economic disruptions. The presence of a military force or base in a city expands the demand for businesses to cater to soldiers.

Some women and girls become prostitutes voluntarily, knowing at the time they are recruited that sex work will be involved, but unaware that they are facing slavery with no income and deplorable work conditions. Others are involuntarily recruited when they are kidnapped, deceived, or coerced. Some girls are raped and then, no longer virgins and pure for marriage, coerced to become prostitutes. Sometimes women are tricked by being told that they are being hired for domestic or factory work; then they are trapped in brothels they cannot escape. Debt bondage traps women when a parent or husband (sometimes from sham marriages to men who marry them to enslave them) sells them into indentured labor, and they are then required to work as prostitutes to pay back the "debt" from the cost of travel, payoffs, and living and healthcare expenses. They have no idea how much they owe, the debt continues to increase, and eventually it becomes clear that they will never be able to repay their debt. Their passports and other identification are usually confiscated; they are isolated in countries where they do not speak the language or know their way around; they have no access to healthcare, food, or basic needs other than through the brothel owners, and they have no money of their own.

Sex Tourism

One of the industries that is supplied by human trafficking is sex tourism. Traveling in Asia to conduct research on sexual slavery, David Batstone describes what he observed in the streets of Bangkok at night. "Middle-aged men walk hand-in-hand with teenage girls. These sex tourists have traveled from all over the world to be here and play out their own private fantasy. Some men pay for quick sex, but most prefer to buy a 'girlfriend' for an entire night or even several days. The johns behave like young adolescents, publicly pawing their 'dates,' squeezing their buttocks and breasts with little shame."

Travel agencies all over the world advertise "exotic sexual adventures" with Asian women "who know how to please a man." Batstone cites a survey of travel agents, conducted by the international aid agency World Vision, that found that 65 percent of all tourists to Cambodia are men and one-fifth of them arrange their trips for the express purpose of having sex. Approximately two-thirds of foreign visitors entering Thailand were unaccompanied men.

Sex tourism thrives in several regions, but its largest growth has been in Asia. Prostitution is not new to Asia, but it has developed as an industry in part because of U.S. military bases and R&R (rest and recreation) centers established in Southeast Asia and the Philippines during several wars, especially the Vietnam War. The variety of recreational services established for American troops, such as bars, clubs with dancing or entertainment, massage parlors, and baths—as well as sales of drugs and pornography—were easily adapted for international tourism in peacetime. Tourism has grown as a means to increase foreign revenue for many countries, and it has expanded economic development by foreign investors and multinational corporations. As discussed earlier in this chapter, this kind of development increases the wealth of the wealthiest and the profits for foreign investors, but it does not relieve the extreme poverty in the region. Sex tourism also thrives in this particular region because of racist attitudes of Westerners about Asian women and girls. Seen as "exotic" (mysteriously different from Western women, naturally submissive and subservient, "geisha girls" who are experts at and enjoy pleasing men), they are sexualized and dehumanized. The realities and conditions of their lives, their individuality, their roles as daughters and mothers, and the economic and cultural forces that lead them to prostitution are invisible.

Young girls (children) are increasingly sought in Southeast Asia and some other areas because of the demand for virgins by tourists who fear AIDS, and by men from some Asian cultures who believe that sex with a virgin brings luck in new business ventures. Organized pedophile networks in Western countries that operate via the Internet have also contributed to sex tourism with children.

Women and children do occasionally escape from enslavement, and they have been assisted by a growing number of activists and organizations that are compiling information, educating the public, influencing public policies, and opening safe houses and shelters to protect victims of trafficking. Many women and children have been safely repatriated to their homes. The first shelter for women and children victimized by trafficking and domestic violence was opened in Laos in 2006; it is operated by the Asia Foundation and supported by UNICEF and the Japanese Embassy in Laos. It provides shelter and counseling to fifty women and children, and it plans to teach job skills to help victims become self-sufficient. Elsewhere, in Myanmar, Save the Children UK (working with local nongovernmental organizations, World Vision, the International Organization for Migration, and the UN Interagency Project on Human Trafficking) has recruited and trained returned trafficked victims to work as volunteer peer educators.

Culturally Unique Forms of Violence Against Women

Although violence against women is a multidimensional phenomenon, with social, psychological, and economic components, in every part of the world it is also linked to values, beliefs, and social norms. Cultural and religious beliefs differ by region and community. As global communications interconnect the world, we have become increasingly aware of the commonalities and differences among cultures. Migrations of people worldwide and the immigration to the United States and Europe of people from Africa, Asia, and South and Central America have created tremendous diversity among people in U.S. and European cities, and many of them maintain cultural practices from their countries of origin even as they adapt to their new countries. The presence of aid workers in poverty-stricken and war-torn countries has exposed practices that are judged internationally as human rights violations against women. This exposure has challenged traditional oppressive culturally unique forms of violence against women.

It is not culture itself that dictates whether women are beaten, raped, or killed, but it is those who control the right to speak on behalf of culture. The rise in fundamentalism all over the world, including the United States, has led to interpretations of traditional practices and beliefs that are more extreme in oppression of women because of fundamentalist views about virginity, chastity, and women's subservient roles in relation to men. Intimate partner violence, sexual assault, sexual harassment, and sex trafficking are culturally and socially based crimes against women that occur all over the world, and they are recognized by Western feminists as similar to Western women's experiences in spite of cultural and national differences. Other forms of violence against women that are unique to particular communities or groups, wherever they occur, are less familiar to people from Western Europe and the United States. Some prominent examples are female genital cutting, honor killings, and dowry deaths.

Female Genital Cutting

Female genital cutting and female circumcision are terms used for procedures that surgically alter a woman's vagina and/or labia for nonmedical reasons as part of traditional rites of womanhood. People who campaign against it often call it "female genital mutilation" because of the harm it causes. It has been practiced for centuries all over the world by several different ethnic, cultural, and religious groups, in twenty-six African countries and in some Middle Eastern and Asian countries, and in immigrant communities in the United States, Europe, and South America. Practitioners include Muslims, Christians, Falashi (Ethiopian) Jews, and followers of indigenous African religions. In fact, in countries where the practice is prevalent, such as Ethiopia, it is practiced by all religious groups, including Protestants, Catholics, Copts, Jews, Animists, and others.

The actual procedures and the meaning of rituals and practices vary from one group to another. The girls' age, which type of procedure is

Fatma's Story

Twenty-four-year-old Fatma Ibrahim told the *New York Times* in 2007 that she was eleven years old when she was taken to a doctor for what her parents described as "a blood test." She was put to sleep, she says, and upon waking she found herself unable to walk. Though Ibrahim believes her parents "'will kill' her if they find out," she has responded to her experience by becoming active in Egypt's movement against genital cutting.

performed, and how it is performed depend on what country the girl lives in, which ethnic and religious group she belongs to, her family's socioeconomic status, and whether she lives in a rural or urban setting. The procedures may be performed individually, by doctors in clinics, or in groups, by elder women in the community or midwives. A girl may be circumcised any time between her birth and her first pregnancy, though it most commonly occurs between ages four and nine. It is estimated that 85 million to 120 million girls have undergone genital surgeries. There are an estimated two million new surgeries every year.

The mildest form, which consists of a slight nicking of the genitals with a sharp instrument, poses few if any health risks. The more serious forms, clitoridectomy and infibulation, often involve extreme pain and pose serious health risks. Medical complications can include hemorrhaging, septicemia, shock, urinary tract or kidney infections, pelvic infections, cysts and abscesses, scarring, menstrual pain and blockage, infertility, and even death. Sexual intercourse and vaginal exams can be difficult or painful, and complications can arise during childbirth. Some women experience difficulty in urinating, incontinence, or difficulty in achieving penetration during sex. Many women who undergo female genital cutting lose sexual function. Excision of the clitoris is likely to impair a woman's ability to achieve orgasm.

Men and women in communities in which female genital cutting is practiced believe that women must be virgins when they marry, and that female sexuality is dangerous because of women's natural

Types of Female Genital Surgeries

According to the 1999 World Health Organization report *Female Genital Mutilation Programmes to Date*, there are four types of female genital surgeries:

- Surgeries that remove the clitoral hood (the prepuce), with or without part or all of the clitoris
- Clitoridectomy, in which the clitoral hood and clitoris are excised along with part or all of the labia minora
- Infibulation, in which the external genitalia are excised and the vaginal opening is sewn partly shut; a small hole is left to allow urine and menstrual blood through, and the hole is reopened when the girl marries (this type of surgery is the most severe, least practiced, and most studied of the four)
- Other types of ritual changes to women's genital areas, such as piercing, stretching, cauterization, or scraping

promiscuity and the harm they can cause to the honor of the family and the purity of the lineage. Clitoridectomy and infibulation aim to inhibit women's sexual desire, to guarantee their virginity, and to maintain sexuality for reproductive purposes only. Girls who have not undergone genital cutting are considered unmarriageable, which has the harsh economic and social consequences that unmarried women face. Women's economic status depends on marriage, not only in terms of income, but also in terms of long-term economic protection and security throughout childbearing years and old age. The pain that girls endure is considered preferable to being a social outcast and unable to marry. The importance of being socially acceptable is powerful, and it motivates parents to have their daughters circumcised to conform to their social strata. It is also an important rite of passage that mothers and grandmothers have endured with dignity, and in the social environment in which they live, it is valued and gives girls social status that is essential to their participation in their communities. This sense of value becomes especially important in cultures where there are few opportunities for women to be so honored, celebrated, and recognized.

Female genital cutting is often justified as a religious practice based on the Judeo-Christian Bible or the Islamic Koran. However, experts on these religions find no writings that support it, and they see these beliefs as existing before the religions originated, perpetuated by interpretations by religious leaders invested in maintaining systems of male domination. Similarly, parts of the Koran and Bible that support women's value, equality, and partnership with men are often selectively ignored or interpreted to fit social and political values.

There are other beliefs that support female genital cutting. Inaccurate beliefs about anatomy perpetuate it—for example, the idea that the clitoris is male and must be removed or it will grow to the size of a penis, or the belief that having sex with a woman who has been circumcised will keep a man from getting HIV/AIDS. Some believe that the practice maintains female cleanliness, and others believe that it increases fertility.

Female genital cutting is seen by feminists and activists as symbolic rituals that aim to subordinate women to their husbands and to the purity of the patrilineage into which they marry. But a 2005 *Harvard Civil Rights–Civil Liberties Law Review* article by law professor Nancy Ehrenreich and Mark Barr points out that while it is important to acknowledge that female genital cutting is part of a complex patriarchal system of male domination of women and a harmful health problem, it is also true that the procedure "has not traditionally served solely as a way for women to get husbands or for men to control women's sexuality." Instead, the authors write, it has a "role in creating bonds among women, in forging a sense of identification with one's group, and in serving as an age-group ritual of camaraderie and bravery."

"Through this lens," the article continues, "practitioners of female genital cutting are seen as individuals who are trying to help parents improve the chances of life success and happiness of their children, not just as misogynists trying to control women." Discussions of female genital cutting by Western activists have conveyed attitudes that characterize the cultures in which it is practiced as ignorant, barbaric, primitive, and misogynist, and they have used punitive approaches to "abolish" it rather than "eradicate" it. They have ignored similar Western practices, such as intersex cutting (performed on babies born with ambiguous genitalia) and cosmetic genital enhancement surgeries aimed at producing "designer vaginas."

From an intersectionalist viewpoint (the perspective that culture, race, class, and gender are not completely separate but interact with one another to make experiences qualitatively different), though, female genital cutting is not just a problem of difference in culture or religion or of gender but a human rights and public health concern as well. It is a violation of women's human rights to freedom from discrimination, high standards of health care, physical integrity, and autonomy. It presents serious health risks to many of the women who experience it, causing health problems that can be prevented. Bearing these issues in mind, the United Nations and activists and governments in a number of Middle Eastern and African nations are using less coercive, less judgmental, and more education-focused policies for long-term social change that are respectful of local cultures and religions.

Female genital cutting is illegal in many countries, even though it is tolerated and practiced widely. It has been against the law in the United States since 1996. It has been the subject of several international treaties and declarations. At least fourteen countries in Africa have banned female genital cutting. In 2003, the Pan African Committee on Traditional Practices met in Ethiopia; delegates from thirty countries attended and declared zero tolerance for the practice. It has been condemned by the United Nations, prohibited in several European countries and effectively banned in others, and made illegal in the majority of countries where it is commonly practiced. Changes in government policies have provided the public structure for taking female genital cutting seriously.

Culturally responsive and indigenous activists are engaging in localized educational programs to keep the public policies from making the practice more secretive and hidden and to more effectively promote changes in the cultures that practice it. Many communities have replaced the practice of female genital cutting with a coming-of-age ceremony: for example, in Kenya, some communities have adopted an alternative rite of passage, replacing female genital cutting with a rite called "Ntanira na Mugambo" ("Circumcision Through Words"). It began in 1996 when thirty families from Gatunga village in Tharaka (two hundred miles east of Nairobi) verbally initiated their daughters into womanhood. The rite brings young girls together for a week in seclusion, where they receive lessons about reproduction, hygiene, personal health, self-esteem, communication skills, and their roles as women. The week ends with a graduation ceremony, where the community comes together to celebrate the girls' coming of age.

Honor Killings

In countries such as Brazil, Egypt, Jordan, Pakistan, and Turkey, communities tolerate and condone "honor crimes." They are rare, but they often result in death. It is difficult to know the extent of honor killings because they often occur within the privacy of the family, and because they are not reported. The UN Population Fund attempted to count honor killings in fourteen countries and found that up to five thousand women are killed each year. Of these five thousand, one thousand to fifteen hundred are estimated to occur in Pakistan (accounting for those not reported as well). At least 565 women and girls in Pakistan died in honor killings in 2006, according to the Human Rights Commission of Pakistan—nearly double the number it recorded the year before. Honor killings accounted for one-third of the reported murders of women in Jordan in 1999. Some believe that the number of honor killings in countries that practice it has risen with more awareness and modernization: young women are exposed to modern culture, and fall in love, behave with more freedom, or

Sahe's Story

Tracy Wilkinson wrote about twenty-one-year-old Sahe Fidan in a *Los Angeles Times* article in January 2007. Fidan, miserable in a marriage to a husband she hated, left him and fled to her parents; they turned her away, telling her, "A married woman can leave her husband only in a coffin." Fidan did return home, and soon afterward, she was discovered in the bathroom, hanged. Her infant son had been tied to her back. "Fidan may have joined the ranks of Turkish women forced to kill themselves, or whose slayings are disguised to look self-inflicted," Wilkinson writes. "The killing of women and girls by male relatives who think the females have brought shame to the family's honor is an atrocity that has plagued Turkey and other countries for generations." As part of Turkey's efforts to join the European Union, the government has initiated a major campaign to end honor killings.

experience sexual assaults, and these often result in clashes with fathers who punish their daughters' "shameful" behavior.

According to Amnesty International, there are three main reasons women are killed by their families: for choosing a marriage partner, for seeking divorce, and for being raped. Choosing one's own marriage partner is seen as a defiant act in communities where most marriages are arranged by fathers. The marriage is therefore not considered valid, and ensuing sexual relations are seen as outside of marriage, which in Pakistan leads fathers to bring daughters to court under charges of *zina*—unlawful sexual relations. In Iraq, activists believe that honor killings are sometimes a cover for intimate partner violence—for example, when a woman tries to flee an abusive husband and is seen as bringing shame on the family for leaving, or when a woman is killed by a violent husband, and then the claim is made that she was killed because she committed some act that brought shame to the family.

Women are seen to embody the honor of the men to whom they "belong," and the purity of the family line is protected with harsh consequences for jeopardizing it. Therefore, men must guard women's virginity and chastity. (In an extreme example of a familiar double standard, men usually go unpunished for "illicit" relationships, whereas women are killed on the rumor or perception of impropriety.) When a woman is perceived to have had an "illicit" sexual relationship, she violates her family's and her husband's family's honor; in many communities, the punishment for this is death. A man's ability to protect his honor is judged by his family and neighbors, and he demonstrates his power to safeguard and restore his honor by killing any who damage it.

Whether or not a woman consents to any behavior that is considered to cause family shame is irrelevant to those whose role is to guard family honor. Consequently, a woman brings shame on her family if she is raped. Going to the police to report rape is often considered to bring dishonor to the family, and victims may be killed for doing so. In some cases, women may even be physically punished for the sexual indiscretions of male relatives. In one widely publicized instance in Pakistan, Mukhtaran Bibi, a thirty-year-old member of the Gujjar tribe, was raped by four men as punishment for her brother, who had been seen with an unchaperoned woman from the Mastoi tribe. She fought back and testified against the men, resulting in their conviction.

Although practices such as honor killings are sometimes seen as based on fundamentalist religious beliefs about women and their sexuality, tribal community structures and traditions go deeper than religion, as NPR reporter Anne Garrels reported in December 2005. A man who killed his sixteen-year-old cousin in Iraq after she had been kidnapped for several days and returned to her family said he would do it again. "To have let her live would have been worse," he said. "Her life would have been turned into hell." She'd have been imprisoned in her home, he said, and her father wouldn't have been able to face others. No one had asked his cousin what happened to her while she was being held by the kidnappers; no one spoke to her at all, not wanting to be affected by her shame. Men who have been kidnapped are celebrated and welcomed back to their families; women and girls have to live with (or die from) shame from the possibility that while they were among men they might have been raped.

Governments do very little to protect women from honor killings. Police in North African and South Asian countries with this tradition, such as Jordan and Pakistan, often take the side of the man or murderer. If actually tried in court, perpetrators get light sentences. In Jordan, families often select young brothers to commit murder, since they receive even lighter sentences. In its report on honor killings, Amnesty International notes that there is nowhere in their communities for women threatened with honor killing to hide. There are few women's shelters, and any woman attempting to travel on her own is a target for abuse by police, strangers, or male relatives hunting for her. For some women, suicide appears to be the only means of escape. One of the few places where a woman is safe is in the home of a tribal *sardar* (leader), with a *pir* (holy man), or in a religious shrine. While women can obtain protection against honor killings in these refuges, they must conform to strict social roles, which for many of these women means working for years as unpaid servants, and sometimes being abused, in the homes of the *sardar*s.

In Jordan and Pakistan, the only safe refuge is in prison, in "protective custody." If an unmarried woman becomes pregnant, for example, she will turn herself in to the police, and they'll imprison her to "protect her life." In other parts of the world, the person who is threatening someone's life is put in prison, but in Jordan and elsewhere where honor killing is practiced, the threatened victim goes to jail. Most of these women are held indefinitely. They are not charged, and they cannot make bail. If the family bails them out, it is to kill them. So these women waste their lives in prison.

Although attitudes and practices change slowly, local activism on behalf of women in countries in which honor killing occurs is flourishing. Turkey, Pakistan, and other countries have recently passed laws to make honor killings illegal and to make sentences for perpetrators more serious. In Pakistan, the Protection of Women Bill was passed in 2006 to make prosecution of sexual assault cases easier.

The bill dropped the death penalty for people found to have had sex outside marriage, though they could face a five-year prison term. In Jordan, King Abdullah has asked the prime minister to amend all laws that discriminate against women. However, this request did not include providing safe refuge other than prison for women threatened with honor killing.

Dowry Deaths

Paying and accepting dowry has been illegal in India for more than forty years, but the practice is still rampant. The BBC's Lucy Ash reported on dowry in India in 2003; she spoke to Ranjana Kumari, who runs seven domestic violence shelters in Delhi, and who estimates that fights over dowry result in up to seventy deaths and serious injuries a month. "Sometimes women are tortured to squeeze more money out of their families and in extreme cases they're killed," she told Ash. "Then the husband is free to remarry and get another dowry."

If the groom or husband and his family are not satisfied with the wife's dowry, they may humiliate, harass, and physically abuse her. Wives have been confined to their houses, beaten, poisoned, and subjected to unimaginable brutality. A Bangalore-based women's group called Vimochana estimates in Ash's BBC piece that three to five women per day arrive at the city hospital's burns unit suffering from massive burns. "Bride burnings" of women by a husband's family are often reported as kitchen accidents, since many households use kerosene stoves.

Many victimized wives see no alternative but to stay in their husbands' households. This is the only option they believe they have in a society that does not accept divorce and where husbands can retaliate with impunity. Attitudes that stigmatize unmarried or divorced women convince many families to give in to dowry demands, even if it leads to financial ruin. They don't expect legal redress because offenders are usually acquitted when families do take their cases to court. One study reported that out of 799 cases of dowry death taken to court, there was only one conviction.

India's National Crime Record Bureau statistics show that husbands and in-laws killed 7,026 women in 2005 over "inadequate" dowry payments. One dowry death is reported every seventy-seven minutes. This problem cuts across all social and class lines, affecting rich and poor, educated and illiterate, urban and rural. Anti-Dowry Acts were passed in the early 1960s in India and Bangladesh, but they are rarely enforced.

The practice of dowry in India and Bangladesh goes back thousands of years in Hindu marriage traditions. There are two traditional aspects of dowry. *Stridhan* (literally "woman's property") was given directly to the bride by her family and was meant to be an asset to her in times of adversity. Under Hindu law, it was her own property, with full right to dispose of as she wished, and it was passed on to her daughters. Its original intent was to equip a woman for her new life with gifts of bedding, clothing, furniture, or utensils, and to be a consolation for daughters not being included in the inheritance process. The second aspect, *dakshina,* was a gift given out of affection from the family of the bride to the groom; it included any gifts made after the marriage. This usually consisted of gold or cash, in accordance with the family's financial ability. In earlier times dowry was voluntary, and the amount or lack of the gift did not interfere with the completion of a marriage. The dowry system was originally intended to provide security to, and celebrate, a newly married couple in their new life together.

Dowry gradually changed, and the custom came to represent an obligatory gift to the groom's family, required to finalize a marriage for wealthy families, rather than a gift to the couple. It was not until the mid-nineteenth century that ordinary families became socially obligated to provide elaborate dowries, especially families trying to improve their social status. It became so important a custom that the cost might ruin a family—or an insufficient dowry might stop a marriage. As intercaste mixing in schools and jobs has increased, families of lower-status girls have tried to improve their status by marrying their daughters to higher-status husbands (for example, men who are wealthy or professionals with substantial incomes), and the practice of dowry has become commercialized as grooms and their families try to improve their wealth by demanding excessive dowries from families that are desperate to enter the superior class. Meanwhile, *stridhan* has disappeared and is no longer practiced.

Since India opened up to foreign investment in 1990, the country has seen a rise in dowry-related violence alongside its economic boom. The numbers of reported dowry deaths surged from four hundred a year in the mid-1980s to fifty-eight hundred a year in the mid-1990s, according to a 2001 report in *Time* magazine, and the number may be even greater because government statistics account for only a fraction of the total number of dowry killings.

The fact that more people are coming forward to report the crimes accounts for only a part of this increase. "A new acquisitiveness permeates society," reports *Los Angeles Times* staff writer Henry Chu in September 2007, "with more consumer and luxury goods showing up on store shelves and in television commercials." In 2006, Delhi Commission for Women member Varsha Jah told the *International Herald Tribune,* "Everyone is becoming more and more Westernized; they want expensive clothes, they want the consumer objects which are constantly advertised on television. A dowry is seen as an easy way to get them." In many cases, the bride is pressured for more cash, jewelry, and expensive consumer items well past the wedding day.

Dowries have become such a burden that many families avoid having girls. In all castes, because girls are not expected to work—and even if they actually do work—they represent costs to the family without the return a son is expected to bring when he is old enough to support his parents. Women are viewed as a financial drain. Infant mortality for female babies is 40 percent higher than that of male babies. Poverty is the main reason, but dowry is the second. Pregnant women can determine the sex of the baby with ultrasound technology and abort the female fetuses. The 2001 census showed that there are just 933 women for every thousand men in India. Legislation against sex determination tests was passed ten years ago, but the practice is still widespread. A 2006 UN report estimated that female infanticide and sex-selective abortions account for ten million "missing" Indian girls over the past twenty years.

Domestic violence was criminalized in the country in 1983, but generally, abused women who are economically dependent on their husbands have been afraid of the repercussions of turning their abusers in. Activists hope that this will soon change. The Protection of Women Against Domestic Violence Act went into effect in India on October 29, 2006. A coalition of women's rights organizations came together in agreement to successfully campaign for this law; it defines domestic violence broadly to include marital rape, emotional abuse, and economic harassment. It specifically targets dowry harassment. It is revolutionary because of its broader definition of domestic violence (beyond physical violence), but also because of the recourse it offers to victims. The new act entitles a wife to a portion of the marital estate, and it guarantees financial assets to women who leave abusive husbands.

Responding to Violence Against Women: Criminalization and Beyond

Governments have made tremendous progress in criminalizing forms of violence against women such as forced marriage, forced prostitution, human trafficking, rape, and domestic violence at national and international levels. This is especially true in the United States and Europe, where significant law reforms have redefined rape and domestic violence and increased sentences for rapists and batterers, and comprehensive anti-trafficking laws have recently been passed. Under pressure from activists and health organizations, governments worldwide have recognized their responsibility for prevention, accountability, and services addressing violence against women. International, national, and local laws have had many successful outcomes: funding for services for victims of these crimes; research based on reported and prosecuted cases; changes in policies and protocols to prevent, identify, and intervene in cases of violence and abuse; training for law enforcement, justice, and health professionals; increased numbers of reports and successful prosecutions; and public knowledge about violence against women that is changing norms and attitudes about it.

However, criminalizing violence against women is not enough. In spite of laws against many types of violence against women, there is still widespread acceptance and justification of these acts under religious or cultural beliefs and practices and according to what is considered "normal" in any country or community. In addition, the forms of redress made available to women at the national level can be obtained only within criminal legal systems that tend to be biased against women. Often, women cannot easily get access to criminal justice systems. When seeking assistance from police, they may not be taken seriously, or they may be further abused by the police. In the United States and all over the world, women who have sought justice or protection through criminal legal systems have been exposed to further risk or trauma by having to testify without adequate protection, by having to emotionally reexperience the violence, or by being victimized again by the abuser in retaliation for reporting, often with unjust outcomes. Therefore, women are often reluctant to seek assistance from criminal legal systems, and perpetrators are rarely punished for their violence.

An additional angle to consider is that many forms of violence against women are not criminal—for example, certain forms that do not cause physical injury, such as emotional and financial abuse and neglect of girls' health and education. These are not defined as criminal acts, largely because they are too difficult to clearly define and recognize by law enforcement agencies. A global, and universal, perspective of violence against women is that beyond being a crime against an individual woman, it is a social problem and a violation of human rights.

A number of international laws have addressed violence against women. Women's human rights are listed in treaties, conventions, resolutions, declarations, and guidelines, promoted by either the United Nations or a regional human rights body. Treaties are agreements, formally adopted by national governments, that create legally binding obligations for groups of governments that sign the treaties. Every state that has ratified a human rights treaty must ensure that the human rights of its citizens are protected. This means that the government commits to both avoid and prohibit actions that violate human rights and agrees to undertake positive steps to ensure that such violations do not take place. Under international law, specific enforcement bodies, usually specialized agencies, committees, or rapporteurs, monitor a nation's human rights situation. These bodies also review reports and complaints about human rights violations, generally submitted by nongovernmental organizations (NGOs) but also sometimes submitted by individuals.

In July 1998 in Rome, 120 UN member countries adopted a treaty to establish a permanent International Criminal Court, which actually began on July 1, 2002. Then–UN Secretary-General Kofi Annan expressed hope to deter future war criminals and "ensure that no ruler, no State, no junta, and no army anywhere will be able to abuse human rights with impunity." There was a powerful momentum to institute a permanent court in the aftermath of the international tribunals on the former Yugoslavia and on Rwanda, which tried individuals responsible for the world's most serious crimes against humanity, including massive numbers of rapes and murders of women and children.

As set out by the International Criminal Court, *crimes against humanity* include acts such as enslavement, torture, rape, forced pregnancy, persecution on political, racial, national, ethnic, cultural, religious, or gender grounds, the extermination of civilians, and enforced disappearances—but only when they are part of a widespread or systematic attack directed against a civilian population. Random acts of violence—such as rape, murder, or even torture—may be carried out, perhaps even by soldiers in uniform, but they may not actually qualify as crimes against humanity unless they are systematically carried out against a particular group of civilians.

War crimes include violations of the Geneva Conventions and other serious violations of the laws and customs generally applied in international armed conflict. War crimes are also defined as acts committed in armed conflict "not of an international character" when they are committed as part of a plan or policy or on a large scale.

In 1993, the UN General Assembly adopted the Declaration on the Elimination of Violence Against Women, which (according to Radhika Coomaraswamy) holds states responsible to "exercise due diligence to prevent, investigate and, in accordance with national legislation, punish acts of violence against women, whether those acts are perpetrated by the state or by private persons." This landmark document was the result of efforts of the UN Commission on the Status of Women and the UN Economic and Social Council to address violence against women. As a UN General Assembly declaration, it does not have the binding legal authority of a convention or treaty, but it is universal in coverage and a strong statement of principle to the international community. It declares that states must combat violence against women by prevention and investigation, by developing comprehensive legal, political, administrative, and cultural programs to prevent violence against women, by training law enforcement officials, and by collecting statistics about the incidence of acts of violence against women.

In 1994, the Commission on Human Rights appointed Coomaraswamy, a human rights activist from Sri Lanka, as the first Special Rapporteur on Violence Against Women. She held this position until July 2003, when the commission appointed Yakin Ertürk, a women's human rights expert from Turkey, to the position. The mandate of the special rapporteur is to gather information on violence against women, its causes and consequences, from governments, treaty bodies, specialized agencies, and other special rapporteurs and to recommend measures at the national, regional, and international levels "to eliminate violence against women and its causes and to remedy its consequences." Rapporteurs are seen as one of the most effective tools within the United Nations to monitor human rights violations.

Ms. Ertürk issued a report in 2006 on the due diligence standard as a tool for eliminating violence against women. Under the due diligence obligation of the 1993 UN Declaration, nations have a duty to take positive action to prevent and protect women from violence, punish perpetuators of violent acts, and compensate victims of violence. To fulfill this obligation, nations must "take measures to modify the social and cultural patterns of conduct of men and women to eliminate all practices based on the idea of inferiority or superiority of either of the sexes." This includes supporting such efforts as awareness-raising campaigns and curricula that challenge gender stereotypes and "uncouple masculinity from oppressive uses of power." However, as of now, the application of the due diligence standard has been limited. Although many states have adopted specific legislation and developed awareness education and training programs, there has been no accountability regarding the actual success of intended changes. The failure to exercise due diligence is itself a human rights violation, even in the absence of harm.

Providing asylum to women fleeing gender-based violence is a strategy being tested in the United States and Europe. The Center for Gender and Refugee Studies at the University of California Hastings College of Law is campaigning for asylum for women who escape to the United States because they are threatened with female genital cutting or honor killing. In December 2005, the Ninth Circuit Court of Appeals ruled in *Abebe v. Gonzales* that parents who seek to protect their daughters from female genital cutting may have a well-founded fear of persecution. The court reversed an immigration court's decision to deny the Abebes asylum. The Abebes came to the United States from Ethiopia and filed for asylum in 1993. In 1996, their daughter, Amen, was born while they were waiting for their case to be decided. Amen is a U.S. citizen. When their asylum application was denied, they reapplied, arguing that if they were forced to return to Ethiopia, Amen would have to undergo female genital cutting. More and more appeals court judges are criticizing decisions made by immigration judges denying asylum to women fleeing honor killings, domestic violence, and genital cutting.

Yakin Ertürk concludes that "if we continue to push the boundaries of due diligence in demanding the full compliance of States with international law, including to address the root causes of violence against women and to hold non-State actors accountable for their acts of violence, then we will move towards a conception of human rights that meets our aspirations for a just world free of violence."

Collaging is often used as a therapeutic release for women who have suffered from trauma, violence, or abuse. National nonprofie organizations such as A Window Between Worlds facilitate art workshops as a healing experience for women in shelters, transitional homes, and outreach projects.© Ginny Fleming

CHAPTER 3

CONSEQUENCES

VIOLENCE AGAINST WOMEN DOESN'T AFFECT just individuals and families; it has large-scale ramifications for societies and nations as well. The consequences of widespread violence against women manifest in many different ways: countries, whether industrialized or developing, can't reach their full potential as long as women's potential to participate in society is denied. Violence against women undermines half of the population, affects child survival, and has a negative impact on the viability of the family. A single rape can affect many women; fear of rape leads women to restrict their residences, work, activities, and movements to avoid being raped. It's impossible to know the full effects of this restrictive fear on women's achievement of their potentials, health, and economic well-being.

Social and economic disadvantages to countries with high levels of violence against women are significant. Population problems trouble the governments of China and India, which are experiencing significant shortages in numbers of women because of cultural preferences for male children that result in practices such as femicide (abandoning female children or allowing them to die) and sex selection (determining sex via ultrasound during pregnancy and then aborting female fetuses).

The social costs of violence against women are impossible to calculate. The human cost is invisible—fear and shame prevent many women from speaking out, and data collected worldwide are insufficient and inconsistent. Violence undermines personal relationships and the quality of life for victims, and the health and behavior problems of children who have witnessed violence negatively affect their education and their future capacity to obtain adequate employment. Women who have experienced male violence are often socially isolated, preventing them from participating in community and income-earning activities, as well as voting or otherwise participating in democracy.

In communities where being a victim of rape is highly stigmatized, the social consequences of victimization intensify greatly. Mary Koss, Lori Heise, and Nancy Russo, writing in "The Global Health Burden of Rape," give examples of the social effects of sexual assault in the Middle East and parts of Asia: a woman who has been raped, they write, may find herself divorced by her husband, rejected by her family, or killed by a family member to clear the family's honor. The authors discuss Cambodian culture, where women are sometimes compared to cotton: "Once cotton has fallen in the soil it can never be washed completely clean." On the other hand, the saying goes, "Men are like diamonds, which can be washed if soiled." Religious purification rituals are available for men, but "none are available for women who have been raped." Female rape victims experience no respite from a culturally imposed sense of being tainted.

Health Consequences

In a 1989 interview with the *Los Angeles Times,* U.S. Surgeon General C. Everett Koop declared violence against women to be the biggest public health risk to adult women in the United States, urging the public health community to "respond constructively to the ugly facts of interpersonal violence." Three years later, Surgeon General Antonia Novello stated in the *Journal of the American Medical Association* that violence was the leading cause of injuries to U.S. women ages fifteen to forty-four. These significant public statements helped generate major funding, research, and public health awareness programs, focused on preventing violence against women in the same ways that the U.S. public health system has worked to prevent smoking and breast cancer.

In the United States, Canada, and the United Kingdom, women who have suffered from intimate partner violence and sexual assault use more healthcare services and report worse health status than women who have not been victimized. Girls who undergo the most extreme forms of female genital cutting (circumcision or infibulation) in the United States, Europe, Africa, and parts of the Middle East are at risk for several different health problems at different points in their lives, such as onset of menstruation, first sexual intercourse, or childbirth. Women and girls forced into sex work or sexual slavery are susceptible to serious health problems because the neglectful and abusive conditions in which they live and work expose them to all kinds of infections (including HIV/AIDS and other STDs) as well as injuries from violence. In a 1994 study using data from a World Bank modeling exercise, rape and domestic violence rated higher than cancer, motor vehicle accidents, war, and malaria in a list of ten selected causes and risk factors for disability and death among women between the ages of fifteen and forty-four.

Physical Health

The effects of violence on women's physical health can be serious and long lasting. Injuries resulting from violence can lead to permanent disabilities, chronic pain, or ongoing medical problems. Trauma and stress created by violence and abuse can cause difficulties such as chronic headaches, gastrointestinal problems, muscle pain, or eating disorders. Problems with access to or use of healthcare can add to poor physical health. Women who are abused by partners or who have experienced genital cutting are often reluctant to seek medical care, fearing judgment, exposure, or reports to law enforcement agencies. People involved with committing the violence (such as partners of abused women, or individuals who employ trafficked women for sex work or domestic work) may actively interfere with a woman trying to get to medical treatment. Access to healthcare can also be limited because of factors including income, distance from medical services, lack of transportation or childcare, and inability to take time off from work.

Particular health problems and conditions are linked to particular forms of violence. Following are some of the common physical health risks associated with intimate partner abuse, sexual assault, sexual harassment, forced prostitution, and female genital cutting.

Intimate Partner Violence

In two U.S. surveys, women who were abused by a spouse or live-in partner were significantly more likely than other women to define their health as "fair" or "poor" rather than "good" or "excellent." While this might have been due to physical injuries incurred during assaults, women who have been battered also are more likely to have chronic health problems not directly related to abuse. Relationship abuse is also correlated to health risks such as smoking and alcoholism.

The most obvious health consequence of intimate partner violence, though, is physical injury. In the United States, intimate partner violence is a major cause of emergency room visits, and U.S. studies have shown that a woman is more likely to be injured by an intimate

Health Effects of Teen Dating Violence

In two major recent studies of adolescent health, one in five girls was found to have been physically and/or sexually abused by a dating partner. The studies also found that one in three male and female adolescents had suffered some form of dating violence. Being physically abused preceded unhealthy high-risk behaviors such as:

* Frequent sex with multiple partners
* Not using condoms
* Substance abuse
* Unhealthy weight control behaviors

In addition, the research indicated that pregnancy was twice as likely for abused girls as for nonabused girls, and that abused girls were at increased risk of STDs, depression, and suicide.

partner than any other type of assailant. Injuries might be minor (such as cuts or light bruises), or they may require medical attention or lead to permanent disability. The 2005 National Crime Victimization Survey found that "on average between 2001 and 2005, half (52%) of all females experiencing nonfatal intimate partner violence suffered an injury from their victimization; one-fifth of victims reporting injury sought medical treatment."

Chronic pain is commonly found among women victims of violence. Medical experts Jacquelyn Campbell and Karen Soeken explain that chronic pain can result from somatization—physical symptoms caused by emotional reactions (headaches resulting from stress, for example)—or it can be the result of old, misdiagnosed, or never-treated injuries (for instance, headaches resulting from previous spinal or head injuries).

Most studies show that victims of violence develop a variety of stress-related symptoms, such as headaches, nausea, back pain, irritable bowel syndrome, digestive problems, and eating disorders. Vulnerability to physical illnesses, too, is often caused by stress. Studies find that negative symptoms associated with relationship violence are likely to subside, at least partially, when a woman is no longer being abused.

During pregnancy, intimate partner violence presents a serious health threat to mothers, unborn children, and newborns. Some women report that their abusive partners aim beatings at their stomachs. There is a well-documented connection between abuse during pregnancy and low birthweight of newborn babies. Medical researcher Judith McFarlane reports that in her studies, a small group of women, more likely to be in their first pregnancy, said that their husbands were jealous of their normal increasing attachment to their unborn child. Another small group had partners who thought the baby wasn't theirs. The largest group said that their abuse during pregnancy was just a continuation of abuse that occurred before the pregnancy.

Anita's Story

Anita's boyfriend, Jimmy, beat her worse when she was pregnant. He always aimed for her stomach and the back of her head. His angry outbursts usually occurred when he thought she was looking at another guy. Because of his jealousy and his violence during the pregnancy, she broke up with him. Two weeks before her baby was due, she visited a friend, and Jimmy was there. As soon as he saw her, he grabbed her, held her, and wanted to have sex. When she refused, he got mad, and pushed her, hard. She fell straight backward, screaming with pain. The next day, she had the baby.

Sexual Assault

Health problems are common among women who have been sexually assaulted. The physical consequences of sexual assaults by strangers, acquaintances, or intimate partners include pregnancy and sexually transmitted diseases (including HIV/AIDS). Untreated STDs can lead to pelvic inflammatory disease (PID), which can cause infertility. Nongenital physical injuries from being raped may be minor, or they may cause permanent disabilities. Sexual assault can also result in PID, vaginal and anal tearing, bladder infections, sexual dysfunction, chronic pelvic pain, urinary tract infections, and other genital and urinary health problems. Unintended pregnancy can also result when an intimate partner uses intimidation to coerce sex and refuses to use protection.

As with other forms of violence, the severe stress and fear caused by sexual assault can result in health problems such as headaches, chronic pain or other nervous system problems, and substance abuse. Research and reports from programs that help female substance abusers with long-term addictions to alcohol, cocaine, heroin, or prescription drugs have indicated that a majority have experienced sexual violence–related trauma.

In places where cultures place extremely high value on virginity, victims of rape may seek surgical reconstruction of their hymens.

Where honor killings result from rape, women are at high risk for murder by family members and for suicide.

Women who have been sexually assaulted may not seek immediate medical assistance, but they are more likely than nonvictims to seek medical assistance in the years after the assault. They report that they are in poor health and complain of limitations in their daily functioning. Sometimes they don't recognize that their symptoms are related to having been sexually assaulted.

Even women who don't want to report rape or are pressured not to tell anyone about having been raped do seek medical care, immediately after the rape and/or later, for help with lingering effects. In a study conducted by a health maintenance organization, 22 percent of women enrolled who had a history of rape or childhood molestation visited a doctor ten or more times a year, compared with 6 percent of nonvictimized women. In this study, repeated visits to doctors were

Nicole's Story

Nicole's stomach ached all the time, and no matter how hungry she was, she couldn't make herself eat. She went on a vacation to visit relatives, and afterward she realized that the whole time she'd been away, her appetite had returned and her stomach didn't hurt. She'd felt better than she had for a year. Back home, when her stomach started hurting again, she realized what caused it: she was terrified of her neighbor, who had sexually assaulted her a year ago. She had known him for a long time, but not very well. He had manipulated her to help him with a problem he was having, and then he wouldn't let her leave his house. He raped her, and then he made her swear not to tell anyone. She was afraid of what would happen if she reported him. She knew her immigrant family would be afraid of the police. She also knew they would think it was her fault and tell her not to ruin his life. She also knew she should see a doctor, because sometimes her stomachaches were like shooting pains in her pelvis. She tried not to think about it.

most likely for women who experienced the most severe violence. Severity of violence was the most powerful predictor of total yearly doctor visits and outpatient medical costs, more than age, ethnicity, self-reported symptoms, and serious injurious health behaviors. By studying how frequently these women saw doctors for five years before and after being sexually assaulted, the researchers determined that they saw doctors more frequently only temporarily, after the sexual assault. The use of healthcare was highest in the second year after the sexual assault, which indicates that the women had chronic persisting health problems rather than acute injuries.

Sexual Harassment

Nausea, headaches, and exhaustion are the most common physical symptoms reported by victims of sexual harassment. In addition, harassment victims have reported debilitating stress, stomach problems, jaw tightness and teeth grinding, binge eating or other disordered eating, inability to sleep, tiredness, and crying spells. Health problems are more common for women who have experienced more severe types of victimization, such as rape or attempted rape. Chronic or situational physical health problems connected to sexual harassment are most commonly related to the severe stress resulting both from the harassment itself and from the consequences (such as the reporting process, retaliation, isolation, and fear).

Forced Prostitution

Women and girls forced into prostitution or trafficked into sexual slavery suffer all kinds of health problems and do not receive healthcare when they need it. "Nu," trafficked from Thailand to Japan, told her story to the Coalition Against Trafficking in Women after escaping from a brothel. Her experiences were typical of women forced into prostitution. She "entertained" multiple clients every night. The girls at her brothel couldn't refuse to see a client. The clients were often violent, Nu said, and would sometimes beat the girls badly before sex. "If girls came back traumatized after a sadistic client and reacted

Monique's Story

Monique complained to her doctor that she was having trouble breathing and had been coughing for weeks, but she didn't feel that she was sick. She admitted that she had started smoking, more than a pack a day, and was extremely tense all the time. Her girlfriend woke her up at night because she made so much noise—grinding her teeth, coughing, and restlessly moving. She joked that her girlfriend was going to leave her if she didn't get better, and then she burst into tears. Barely able to speak, she told her doctor that a senior manager at work had repeatedly gotten her alone, groped her, and told her that he couldn't keep his hands off her. She had put a lot of time into this job and she loved her work, so she hadn't told anyone what was happening.

hysterically . . . they would be beaten by the mamasan and told they must have provoked the client to be violent," she said. "If we cried on the job or resisted a client we were beaten even more." Nu, like many other women in her situation, used drugs to numb the pain.

Under these conditions, clients usually refuse to use condoms. Pregnancy may lead to more beatings and abuse. Abortions are often self-induced with the help of women in the brothels. Girls often don't know about STDs or HIV/AIDS, and many become infected.

Living and working conditions are often squalid, crowded, and unhealthy. Women are often underfed and malnourished. They may become pale and weak because they are not allowed outdoors. They may have multiple injuries from rape and beatings. They may develop multiple health problems, such as frequent infections, fever, stomachaches, nervousness, or mental breakdowns. Some attempt suicide. It is common to have painfully bad teeth; women sometimes pull their own teeth or lose them. Doctors' visits are usually allowed only when women suffer from severe symptoms, and the cost is most often added to the overwhelming debt that they have to pay off by prostitution.

Female Genital Cutting

Girls who have undergone circumcision or infibulation may experience medical complications such as shock; severe bleeding (sometimes leading to death); tetanus; wound infections; urinary tract, pelvic, or kidney infections; septicemia; cysts or abscesses; formation of large amounts of scar tissue; and lengthy, painful convalescence. If the procedures have been performed by individuals with little or no modern medical training, under nonsterile conditions, and without the benefit of anesthesia, health risks are greater.

After recovery, medical problems—chronic urinary tract or bladder infections, difficulties passing urine or menstrual blood, incontinence, scarring, menstrual pain and blockage, and infertility—may continue. Upon marrying, infibulated women must have their stitches cut open to permit intercourse, or they have them opened by attempts at intercourse through time. The ensuing difficulty achieving penetration during sex, or the tearing that results, can be painful. Infibulation may make it difficult for women to obtain vaginal exams. Excision of the clitoris is likely to severely impair a woman's ability to achieve orgasm. Painful scarring and infections can also limit the enjoyment that a woman can expect to attain from sexual relations. Vaginal penetration can be so difficult that some couples resort to anal intercourse. At the time of the birth of the woman's first child, the opening must be cut further to allow passage of the baby's head. Prolonged and obstructed labor may occur during childbirth. Painful scar tissue may form.

Mental Health

It is common for women to experience mental health symptoms after assault and abuse, and women seek healthcare services for these as frequently as for physical health problems. Every study of the health consequences of violence against women has found that the primary reason victims visit a primary healthcare setting (e.g., a doctor's office, health clinic, or hospital) is clinical depression. Depression and suicide attempts are four times more likely in female victims of severe intimate partner violence than in nonvictimized women. Depression most often stems from the frequency and severity of current or recent violence/abuse and stress, not from emotional problems or mental illness that existed before the violence.

An exception to this is the violence experienced by seriously mentally ill women—for example, those who have schizophrenia, bipolar disorder, or serious depression. Because of their disabilities and periodic difficulties dealing with realities of daily life or functioning, they are especially vulnerable to exploitation, abuse, and violence, and their symptoms are likely to be worsened or complicated by being traumatized by violence.

Women tend to feel responsible for their own victimization—no matter what form it takes—believing that they somehow provoked it or should have been able to prevent it, which contributes to depression, low self-esteem, and self-blame. If people around them—family, friends, neighbors, coworkers—respond by questioning how they happened to be victimized or blame them for doing something to cause it (or for not doing something to prevent it), then their own self-blame becomes worse. Victims of crimes in general try to manage their loss of control and helplessness by repeatedly reviewing the experience and in hindsight figuring out what they did wrong or should have done. This is natural, but it also shifts the focus away from the perpetrator's responsibility and blames the victim. Depression often results when a victim becomes angry with herself rather than with the perpetrator.

Often, women who have survived sexual violence are affected by significant people in their lives who continue to blame them for the violence. Women who do not think they have done anything wrong may begin to search for some answer about why this happened to them when religious leaders or family members question them or accuse them of causing the violence. Some husbands, boyfriends, or parents become upset or obsessed with the wife, girlfriend, or daughter they can no longer see the same way. Other partners or family members become enraged or torment themselves because they were not able to protect the victim and keep her from being hurt or shamed.

Cecilia's Story

Cecilia's aunt was raped in a refugee camp in Thailand after escaping Vietnam after the war. She was a young Chinese teenager (and she looked Chinese). She was raped for several reasons: because she was a young sexualized female, and because of the other refugees' hatred and envy of the Chinese, who were easily able to pay for escape routes from Vietnam. She kept the rape a secret until she met Cecilia's uncle; she felt it was safe to tell this man who loved her so much. However, instead of sympathizing with her pain and understanding her emotional trauma, he was disgusted and developed an intense hatred for her because she wasn't chaste before meeting him. From then on, he constantly verbally abused her for being a "slut," and still does, assuming she had control of the rape and feeling as if it were her fault.

Women who have been traumatized by sexual or physical violence express (and show signs of) feelings of terror and helplessness. Even experiencing nonphysical forms of abuse can leave women with extraordinary levels of dread. Terror is different from fear; fear is a biological response to danger, while terror is a response to a situation from which there is no escape. When we sense danger and are afraid, we become alert, look around, quickly appraise the situation, and fight or flee. This fight or flight response doesn't work in conditions of terror or helplessness, when one perceives no means of escape or way to become safe. Often, a woman's feelings of terror continue after getting away from a rapist, captor, or abuser.

Sexual Assault

Acquaintance rape has a particular impact on women because in the aftermath of the assault, their personal worlds and the world at large may feel very threatening. A substantial number of acquaintance rape victims consider or attempt suicide. They tend to criticize themselves for having poor judgment, not recognizing the rapists' deliberate deception and prior intention to rape them. They often avoid seeking assistance because of shame. Some women choose not to have sex for a while, and others, especially those who felt devalued after the assault, have sex more often than before. Their feelings of trust are uniquely violated. They also are less likely than women raped by strangers to conceptualize the experience as rape.

Psychology researcher Ronnie Janoff-Bulman explains that sexual assault can shatter the basic assumptions people hold about themselves and their world as a reasonably safe and predictable place, populated with people they can trust. Self-blame can be seen as an attempt to make sense of senseless victimization. Janoff-Bulman states that when a survivor of assault asks herself, "Why me?" she "commonly answers this question based on our socialized assumptions about the world being just and predictable: if something bad happens to someone, the victim deserves it either because of his/her personality or his/her actions." If a survivor can perceive herself as the cause of the beating or rape, then rather than having gone through a random, unpreventable occurrence, she can explain to herself what happened, which helps her feel less frightened and helpless. As Andra Medea and Kathleen Thompson note in their book *Against Rape: A Survival Manual for Women: How to Avoid Entrapment and How to Cope with Rape Physically and Emotionally,* "If the woman can believe that somehow she got herself into the situation, if she can make herself responsible for it, then she has established some sort of control over the rape. It was not someone arbitrarily smashing into her life and wreaking havoc." This process is helpful to coping and recovery, but it also may contribute to depression. It is also complicated by responses of others who blame the survivor for her victimization because of their erroneous beliefs about rape or relationship violence or because of their own need to feel that it couldn't happen to them. As explained in Chapter 1, victim blame is inherent in oppressive social structures, and it excuses the perpetrators.

Sexual Harassment

Women who have been sexually harassed often experience deterioration in their emotional or physical condition as a result of their experiences. The more severe the victimization was, the more severe the reactions are. Many women experience strong fear reactions, lowered self-esteem, lessened self-confidence, loss of control, and disruption in their lives. The most common emotional experience of sexually harassed women is of loss: women may lose their jobs, fear losing their jobs, lose coworkers' friendship and support, lose personal dignity, or lose trust in others and confidence in themselves and their future careers or employment. Many women who have been harassed experience humiliation and embarrassment, isolation because of ostracism by coworkers, and hostility and retaliation from those who are accused and supporters of the accused.

Intimate Partner Violence

The ongoing threats, abusive controlling behavior, and intense levels of stress inherent to intimate partner violence can cause long-term reactions of fearfulness, anxiety, and confusion. Women abused by partners commonly experience constant fear, anger, guilt, shame, feelings of powerlessness or helplessness, a sense of failure, and a sense of being damaged or worthless. Many become extremely dependent and find it difficult to make basic decisions or to function alone. Others become easily angered and irritable. Faced with an overwhelming sense of danger, they focus on self-protection and survival. Ending the relationship brings intense grief and feelings of loss.

Intense trauma-based attachments between an abuser and his or her partner make extrication from the relationship especially difficult. In a process known as traumatic bonding, escalating violence can actually increase a person's attachment to an abuser. Strong emotional ties develop between the two people: one person has intense positive feelings for a person of whom she is afraid. The partner who intimidates and is frightening also bonds to and feels dependent on or protective of the victim. Bonding to one's abuser is viewed by many as a survival strategy.

Sara's Story

No one knew about Sara's boyfriend's abuse. Her friends didn't approve of her being with someone eight years older. She hid her bruises with clothing and makeup, and she became more withdrawn. Her closest friends started to notice that she was changing. She blamed herself for the problems: maybe she really was too fat or too ugly, like her boyfriend said. She began exercising a lot and eating less and less. She took diet pills and diuretics. When she did lose weight, she thought he'd be happy. Instead, he told her to wear sweats to school, not show off her body. She kept trying. At times things were good between them, but on bad days, he became violent, hitting her or throwing things at her. Then, when she was upset, he'd apologize, beg her not to leave him, and be her best friend again. She was consumed by him, thinking about him all the time. She couldn't understand how he could be this great guy and then turn into "someone evil."

When one person intermittently harasses, beats, threatens, abuses, or intimidates another, and the badly treated, terrified person perceives him- or herself to be subjugated to or dominated by the other, this dynamic of traumatic bonding can develop. It is based on two features: the power imbalance and the intermittent nature of the abuse (alternately cruel and loving or kind) in the structures of such relationships as abused intimate partner/violent intimate partner, hostage/captor, abused child/abusing parent, cult follower/cult leader, and prisoner/guard. The victim becomes hopeful when the abuser is kind, and she believes he would not want to hurt her. She becomes hypervigilant to his moods and needs, tries to keep him happy, and adopts his views, including seeing people who try to help her as the enemy. She blocks her own feelings of rage and terror, and her own needs, as she struggles to survive by her vigilant focus on the abuser. She experiences a "push-pull" dynamic toward the positive side of the abuser and away from his cruel side that threatens her survival. She feels more and more negative about herself (internalizing his criticism and demeaning of her), incapable of fending for herself, and more dependent on the person with the power.

Traumatic bonding is a normal reaction to hostage conditions in which victims are isolated, terrified that they won't survive, and believe they can't escape, and the abuser or captor shows some kindness to them in the context of terror. Victims of trafficking may experience traumatic bonding as well, if their captors occasionally show caring or positive feelings toward them. *Anyone* would react this way, whatever their previous experiences or vulnerabilities. It is a survival mechanism; law enforcement agencies are encouraged when traumatic bonding develops in hostage situations because when it does, hostages are more likely to survive. When hostages succeed in positively bonding to captors and captors bond to the hostages in turn, captors are less likely to kill the hostages. Understanding this dynamic has also helped to explain how hard it is to end an abusive relationship.

Female Genital Cutting

Long-term psychological effects of female genital cutting procedures may include anxiety, feelings of inadequacy, and depression. Girls may experience trauma reactions or feelings of betrayal. Women may have problems with sexuality later, or a lasting feeling of loss or of having been seriously wounded. While they might feel part of the community of women who have also had this experience, if their life circumstances change, they may have difficult feelings of being different from other women who have not. Expecting people not to understand may interfere socially and may make it especially difficult to seek medical services.

Trauma Reactions

When violence expert Evan Stark reviewed data that he and Anne Flitcraft gathered in the late 1970s from ER medical records of women with injuries associated with relationship violence, he discovered a predictable pattern. "Shortly after an abusive episode," he noted in his 2007 book, *Coercive Control: How Men Entrap Women in Personal Life,* "a woman would typically reappear with a range of medical complaints, then with alcohol on her breath or drug use, then with another injury, a suicide attempt, as depressed or with a presentation of 'nerves.'" He noted that this series of self-destructive behaviors seemed to occur after abusive episodes. He also noted that while all of the patients came to the emergency room complaining of injury, only one injury in fifty was serious enough to require hospitalization. The multiple symptoms indicated that the cases were serious, not from severe violence but from secondary symptoms of complex trauma.

Traumatic events instill feelings of terror and helplessness. Even after the danger is over, the traumatized person continues to respond to specific reminders and to generally threatening situations as though the terrifying event were still occurring in the present. The person's fear system is activated, causing hyperarousal (such as exaggerated startle responses) and hypervigilance. She reexperiences the trauma—for example, by having flashbacks or nightmares. Her response system shuts down, and she may experience numbing, withdrawal, a sense that things aren't real, or a sense of disconnection from herself and others. The traumatized person develops ways of avoiding reminders: she may sleep too much to avoid remembering, not sleep at all to avoid nightmares, use drugs or alcohol excessively, isolate or restrict herself, or psychologically disconnect from reality at times. These are symptoms of post-traumatic stress disorder (PTSD); they can occur after a single traumatizing experience, such as acquaintance or stranger rape. Community studies of adult women have revealed that PTSD is more likely to develop after rape than for any other trauma studied, including other violent crimes and major disasters such as hurricanes.

Repeated trauma, which occurs in any situation of coercive control—for instance, from violence by an intimate partner, repeated rape, or trafficking and forced prostitution—causes a form of post-traumatic stress disorder known as complex PTSD. Studies have found that rates of PTSD among women who seek services for violent relationships range from 40 percent to 80 percent. But in addition to the symptoms of PTSD described above, a person may respond to repeated trauma with a profound passivity in which she gives up initiative and struggle. As psychiatrist Judith Herman, a pioneer in the study of trauma, describes it, complex PTSD affects a person's emotional state as she fluctuates between intense, overwhelming feelings and numbness; in relationships she alternates between desperate dependency and complete withdrawal. One of the long-lasting effects of complex PTSD is restricting relationships and holding back feelings, so the woman becomes withdrawn and shut down. This takes place as a way of coping with intrusive symptoms such as flashbacks or panic attacks from exposure to reminders of the violence.

Substance Abuse

Many women alcoholics and addicts report that they started drinking or using illegal drugs either at the insistence of an abusive partner or to ease the strain of living with him, or to cope with sexual violence. While alcohol and drug use may numb intense emotions and physical pain from injuries, substance abuse also can increase a woman's vulnerability to sexual assault. Often women seek help in substance abuse treatment systems, but they rarely request treatment for current or past sexual or physical abuse trauma. Many studies have shown that victimization rates for lifetime exposure to trauma among women substance abusers is high, ranging from 55 percent to 99 percent. Only recently has the recognition of the interrelatedness of multiple problems made a difference in women getting the help they need for the combination of substance abuse, depression, and trauma.

Recovery from Violence

Judith Herman, in her landmark book, *Trauma and Recovery: The Aftermath of Violence—From Domestic Abuse to Political Terror,* grounds successful recovery in survivors' empowerment. The survivor, she writes, must be the "author and arbiter of her own recovery," and though others "may offer advice, support, assistance, affection, and care," they don't supply a cure. Herman adds, "No intervention that takes power away from the survivor can possibly foster her recovery, no matter how much

Marie's Story

Marie, thirty-one years old, went to a community agency with her two children because she was feeling overwhelmed and depressed. She had been drinking heavily, had lost her housing, and was afraid she was about to lose her job. She found emergency shelter, and she knew she had to deal with her alcohol problem to get on her feet again. But no one asked her about why she was suddenly homeless, and no one knew that she had fled from her violent husband—and she was ashamed to tell anyone.

it appears to be in her immediate best interests." Decreasing a survivor's isolation, expanding her options, and "countering the dynamics of dominance in the approach to the victim" are also important to the process of healing.

Women who have been victimized show many signs of courage and strength, even in the behaviors that may be perceived by others as problematic—for example, carefully planning to escape rather than running from a violent incident. None of us knows how we would manage to keep ourselves going every day after being raped, maybe repeatedly, or being emotionally undermined and controlled. To find safety and to be able to function takes strength in these circumstances.

Herman defines three stages of recovery for survivors: establishing safety, remembering and mourning, and reconnecting with ordinary life. These stages don't take place in a straightforward sequence but occur back and forth through time. The recovery process involves reframing survivors' beliefs that have developed to make sense of the victimization. This includes stopping the belief that they caused or could stop the abuse. Survivors accept personal responsibility for their safety while rejecting personal responsibility for the violence, recognizing the fact that perpetrators choose to use violence, and that they can choose not to.

From an empowerment perspective, survivors of rape or intimate partner violence are mentally healthy adults who have experienced life-threatening crises they had no power to change. In this thinking, while rape and battering crises are manifested by psychological distress or symptoms, the women are not necessarily unhealthy— they have normal responses to terrifying and demeaning experiences. Empowering interventions address women's (and their significant others' and children's) "normal" emotional reactions and the social and cultural context of male violence. Some professional treatment does not address the social context of experiences with male violence. For example, a woman's intense anger may be seen as an emotional problem to be treated, soothed, or medicated, rather than as outrage over vulnerability to male violence that can be helped by peer support groups and empowerment to take some kind of action. Empowerment perspectives also address the underlying structural conditions for independence; although treatment focused on emotional problems can be helpful, it can be disempowering if it is not paired with help to survive independently.

Among the many different resources that help survivors recover are rape crisis centers, emergency and transitional shelters for abused women and their children, shelters and advocacy programs for women who have escaped trafficking and slave labor, and clinics that address female genital cutting and its aftermath.

Rape crisis centers respond to rape survivors in crisis and in the longer-term aftermath of sexual assault. There are rape crisis centers all over the world. They generally offer three basic services: twenty-four-hour hotlines, support groups and individual counseling, and legal and medical advocacy. The hotlines are usually staffed by volunteers and peer counselors, and the counseling services are provided by professionals. Volunteer lawyers or trained advocates help with legal procedures and accompany survivors to emergency rooms, police stations, and courts. Most centers also provide self-defense instruction and public education, advocate for legal and political change, and promote social changes in conditions that perpetuate violence against women.

Shelters for abused women (and their children) have also been established in many countries. They are generally crisis refuges for women fleeing violent situations who have no other place to turn for safety. Transitional shelters provide a place to live for several months while a woman is reestablishing herself after fleeing an abusive relationship; they usually offer survivors healthcare, housing, help to find work, and financial and other support. They operate twenty-four-hour hotlines, support groups, and public education programs, as well as residential crisis intervention services to keep a woman and her children safe while she makes decisions and plans for herself. They also provide legal advocacy to shelter residents and community residents.

Advocacy programs for women who've escaped trafficking and forced labor vary in the scope and nature of services they provide in many countries. Some provide primarily legal services, helping women to be released from detention for illegal immigration, to obtain legal residency status, or to be repatriated safely in their home countries. They also may campaign for legal reforms to stop human trafficking and to eliminate the conditions under which women are vulnerable to trafficking. They provide public education and outreach to vulnerable communities of women and children. The Coalition to Abolish Slavery and Trafficking in Los Angeles is one of the only such programs to provide shelter for women until they can be safe and reestablish their lives.

Under the best of circumstances, recovery from violence can lead to more personally meaningful, better articulated, and more flexible beliefs and confidence in one's strength and courage, as well as improved coping and social supports than experienced before. The recovery process can lead women to feel able to take charge of their lives with increased awareness. Some of the most empowering advocates for women who are recovering from victimization are survivors themselves.

Economic Costs

Violence against women takes an enormous social and economic toll worldwide. It is impossible to actually calculate all of the costs, but a rough picture of how we all pay for the damage it causes can add to our understanding of the magnitude of its scope and consequences and of the urgency of its eradication.

Story Endings

Anita and Jimmy were married, and they hoped to raise their child together. But Jimmy's violence got worse after they were married, and after a year, in spite of her religious beliefs against divorce, and her conflicts with her family about it, Anita ended the marriage. Her struggle and recovery was difficult, but she is now living a life free from violence.

After Nicole realized that her stomach could feel better, she decided to see her doctor, who recommended a counselor. She was relieved that the counselor understood her family's cultural issues about talking about rape. The counselor helped her decide what to do about her family and her neighbor. Gradually, she felt safer and took care of her medical problems. She knows now that her stomach signals her when she is terrified or angry.

Monique found the courage to tell another manager in her company what her senior manager was doing. Supported by this manager, she wrote a letter to the owner of the company, who conducted an investigation. When they found out that the senior manager had done the same thing with other women, they fired him. Monique's been sleeping better since. She talked to the other women and they are all determined that nothing like this will ever happen in silence again.

Sara took women's studies courses in school and became able to see clearly what had happened to her. In a counseling group, she saw how trauma and traumatic bonding had altered her perceptions of herself. She lives with a powerful group of friends now, and she plans to change the world for women like herself.

Marie's recovery took all of her energy for a while, and with the support of a program for women with similar problems to hers, she is putting her life back together. Others tell her daily how much strength she has to stay on her path, and she's proud and grateful.

Direct costs are the actual dollars spent related to violence—for example, the cost of police, courts, judges, social services, healthcare, and mental healthcare. A 2003 report from the Centers for Disease Control and Prevention put the health-related costs of intimate partner violence (rape, assault, stalking, and homicide) in the United States at more than $5.8 billion a year. The costs of providing a year of healthcare for severely victimized women as a group are 2.5 times higher than for nonvictimized women. In the United States alone female victims of violence lose a total of nearly eight million days of paid work and nearly 5.6 million days of household productivity. These costs are for physical health problems. The U.S. Department of Justice estimated that the total annual cost of mental healthcare for victims of attempted or completed rapes is $863 million. Many other costs—for shelter for women and their children, for social services, for police protection, and for judicial and legal services and correctional activities—factor into the ways local and national economies are affected by violence against women. And still other costs are impossible to calculate—for example, the cost to school systems when children who have witnessed violence can't perform well in school, repeat grades, drop out, or need and use services to assist them.

Violence is a key contributor to poverty of women. Many women forced out of the labor market because of violence subsequently fall into poverty. An estimated 25 percent of homeless women are fleeing from abusers. Women are fired from jobs because of problems associated with violence, such as absenteeism, tardiness, lowered productivity, increased security costs, medical expenses, stalking by the abuser after breaking off the relationship, or emotional problems that interfere with work. One study found that only one-third of the battered women the researchers interviewed were able to keep their full-time jobs for six months or longer the year following a report of violence. Many women with jobs, and in the middle class, have financial difficulties because they have spent their savings or had money stolen from them by abusers or rapists. When women work inconsistently because of violence, they may have difficulty maintaining health insurance for themselves and their children.

Employers face financial liability for injuries occurring at work, and assaults in the workplace may victimize other employees as well as the victim of abuse. Employer/employee–sponsored healthcare plans pay for medical costs incurred by incidents of violence. Many battered women do lose their jobs as a result of these factors, from unbearable stress from a partner's interference with her work, or as a result of having to flee from violence.

Indirect costs are losses or costs that are not actually paid for, such as the value of lost productivity, the present value of lifetime earnings for victims who have died from violence perpetrated against them, and losses in educational achievement or career advancement.

Based on 1995 data, the National Center for Injury Prevention and Control (NCIPC) estimates that the value of days lost from paid employment and household chores due to lost productivity because

Merla's Story

During six years of abuse, Merla had missed a lot of work because of beatings, but she'd saved her money, made her plans carefully, and finally moved to her own apartment and filed for divorce. Her husband was enraged, but she was finally safe. What a lifesaver to have a secure job working with people she liked and trusted! Then one day, her husband was in the parking lot at work when she was leaving and yelled at and threatened her. He repeatedly called her at work, begged her to come back, or yelled at her. Then her husband showed up at her workplace and threatened a coworker, accusing him of taking his wife away. Her employer was becoming upset about the danger and disruptions, and Merla was afraid she would lose her job.

Merla's employer sought advice from a legal clinic, obtained a restraining order against Merla's husband, and hired a security guard for the parking lot. Merla was grateful to know that everyone wanted to keep her from losing her job. Her husband realized he wasn't able to intimidate her and was afraid of being arrested again, so he stopped threatening her at work.

of intimate partner violence in the United States is $858.6 million each year, nearly three-quarters of which is due to physical assault. The NCIPC placed the value of lost earnings due to fatal intimate partner violence at $892.7 million. Canada's National Survey on Violence against Women reported that 30 percent of battered wives had to cease regular activities because of abuse, and 50 percent had to take sick leave from work because of injuries. In India, a survey showed that for each incident of violence, women lost an average of seven working days. A study of abused women in Nicaragua found that abused women earn 46 percent less annually than women who have not suffered abuse, even after controlling for other factors that affect earnings.

The picture painted, over and over again, by these statistics, studies, and individual stories, is that violence against women has an incalculably high price. Its costs come directly, in the form of increased healthcare costs, lives lost, and negative effects on women's workforce participation. Indirectly, the human costs take the form of incredible pain and suffering and the disruption of families. When women are violated and live in fear, nations are economically affected by the damage to every country's best resource: a healthy, well-educated population that supports the health, welfare, and development of a nation's future—all of its children.

Poster put out by the Family Violence Prevention Fund. The orgainization's "Coaching Boys into Men" program emphasizes men's responsibility to model respectful attitudes toward women, and to teach boys ways to express anger without using violence. © www.endabuse.org

CHAPTER 4

CONTROVERSIES AND DEBATES

WE ALL HAVE STRONG REACTIONS, values, and emotions about violence against women. As you can see from the first three chapters, issues related to violence against women are complicated and multidimensional. Not only do we study them from multiple points of view (for example, legal, human rights, social science research, psychological, and feminist perspectives), but no one looks at this subject with complete objectivity. Controversies and struggles abound in every country, and debates differ from one country to another. This chapter highlights some of the debates taking place in the United States.

Our conversations about violence against women are shaped by our own experiences, our own ideas (for example, about families and gender), our values regarding what can and should be important, the kind of work we do, and what we study or know most about. The debates and controversies that engage people about this subject are based on two main factors: first, there are so many ways to look at incidents of violence against women that a room full of people who witnessed a violent incident might explain it from as many different points of view as there are people in the room. Second, our perspectives are informed by our particular roles or goals.

Let's start by looking at the people who help victims of violence, and how their goals influence how they respond to what they believe causes violence. Law enforcement agencies, for example, must define illegal violent behavior in a way that makes violations of laws recognizable and enforceable. These agencies have the most clearly documented records of numbers of illegal violent acts, such as rape or assault against an intimate partner, that have been reported (although their records are limited, since not all instances of violence against women are reported). They are clear about observable violence, and their remedies are determined by law. The goal of law enforcement, prosecutors, and courts is to maintain public safety—a narrow focus that can be helpful in arresting and incarcerating offenders and protecting victims.

The goal of psychologists, generally, is to identify and remedy mental disorders. Psychologists and doctors may see the problem of violence against women as caused by psychopathology; they tend to define the issue in psychological or medical terms and seek remedies through medical and psychological treatment.

Activists aim to change society. They may find legal, psychological, and research perspectives to be too limited, and instead they focus on changing the social, economic, and political conditions under which violence against women takes place. Their definitions and ways of identifying problems faced by women often have a broader scope, targeting socioeconomic systems and cultural norms that contribute to violence against women—such as restrictions based on fear of rape, control by husbands and fathers, the criminal justice system's oppression of communities of color, or poverty-driven employment in slavery-like conditions. Although they may respond to individual people who seek help for their problems, the goal of activists and advocates (including survivors of violence) is to promote legal, human, and civil rights of women and to change social systems that tolerate violence against women.

Politicians are responsible for solving problems by creating and changing laws. California State Senator Sheila Kuehl—who has successfully championed twenty-five domestic violence bills—tells about the many controversies she dealt with as a lawmaker: "Mythology [about domestic violence] went, women must bring it on themselves, and, indeed, research was brought forward to show that domestic violence was actually 'mutual combat' with both sides engaged in violent acts. Public policy then developed mutual restraining orders and arrested women for fighting back. . . . Perhaps the most intractable myth influencing public policy was the belief that violence against a parent was not harmful to children [who witness it] unless they, too, were victims of physical violence. This took years of research to change."

The public media, including magazines, television, films, the Internet, and video games, have often been the focus of controversy. Passionate advocates for protection of First Amendment freedom-of-speech rights actively debate those who promote regulation of sexually violent pornography (which many believe leads to desensitization and tolerance for actual sexual violence); both parties call on contradictory research results regarding whether or not men who have viewed violent pornography are more likely to actually commit sexual violence. Music is the focus of similar controversy: rock and hip-hop lyrics that contain violent language, demeaning images of women, and antigay sentiments are defended by some as important artistic expressions of the emotional realities of young people's lives, but they are viewed by others as creating (or at least reflecting and promoting) a culture that celebrates violence, cruelty to women, and homophobia.

Controversies and debates also take place among antiviolence advocates. Women of color activists have been critical of antiviolence movement activism that addresses the issue as if all women were the same, and that makes invisible the realities of violence against women of color. The public information campaign asserting that domestic violence "can happen to anyone" was successful in getting public attention from those who believed that violence happened only to "certain" women—but, as Natalie Sokoloff asserts in her anthology *Domestic Violence at the Margins: Readings on Race, Class, Gender, and Culture,* "Historically white and middle-class feminists sometimes ignored or minimized social differences between women by focusing on a shared . . . victimization among women." Sokoloff quotes feminist activist Ann Russo's statement that the idea of a collective "'sisterhood accomplished just the opposite because it reduced the complexities of many women's stories and it erased our historical, social, and cultural differences and divisions.'"

Perspectives of Women of Color

Activist and researcher Beth Richie, who has studied the relationship between violence against African American women and women's participation
in crime, argues for a reassessment of responses that have been central
to antiviolence work, especially the reliance on law enforcement as prin-
cipal provider of women's safety. Richie and other women of color argue
that while the "anti-violence movement is relying on legal and legislative
strategies to criminalize gender violence, women in communities of color
are experiencing the negative effects of conservative legislation regarding
public assistance, affirmative action, and immigration. And while the antiviolence movement is working to improve arrest policies, everyday safety
in communities of color is being threatened by more aggressive policing,
which has resulted in increased use of force, mass incarceration, and brutality. The conflict between the anti-violence movement's strategy and the
experiences of low-income communities of color has seriously undermined
our work as feminists of color fighting violence against women."

Bessie, a support group facilitator in East Nashville who was interviewed by criminal justice professor Neil Websdale in 1999, expressed her
belief that the women's movement hasn't been able to see that its emphasis on empowerment of individual women does not take into account
black women's concerns with the black community as a whole. (In other
forums, Asian, Hispanic, and Native American battered women have made
similar accusations.) Bessie explained: "One woman said about reporting
to police, 'It's anger about the stigmas, the stereotypes, and the system.'
It's anger about her own situation, but also anger about his situation. The
inner conflict about 'I have to report him and he's a black man. When I
report him, what does that do to him? Then I become part of the system.'
. . . So when sisters come to our program, we are very respectful of them
just for having the courage to pick up the phone."

It is inevitable that clashes and conflicts take place among people
with so many different perspectives and goals. Social movement activists
and professionals in fields such as law enforcement and psychiatry
don't agree on many points, but dialogue and debate among activists,
professionals, politicians, pop culture icons, and others is dynamic and

sustains progress rather than continuing the status quo. The same is true of research that adds to our knowledge about violence against women: researchers who emphasize the importance of gathering women's stories to understand violence often disagree with researchers who study only what is measurable and quantifiable. An atmosphere of controversy and debate challenges our thinking about violence against women; disagreement, analysis, and criticism can sharpen our awareness of complexity and caution us against accepting "facts" at face value.

The dramatic shift in public attention to the forms of violence against women in the United States and worldwide—transforming them from hidden, private problems to the focus of public policy and scrutiny—has led to government intervention and large amounts of funding allocated for services, education, and research. When large amounts of money are involved, debates intensify and become more political. In the political arena, people who have little in common often come together regarding their concerns about violence against women. Law-and-order individuals concerned about public safety and punishing criminals have worked with feminists advocating for changes in the status of women to change criminal laws on rape, domestic violence, and trafficking in women. Politicians and activists have worked together to change laws and eradicate female genital cutting and honor killings.

Though for centuries our culture has accepted myths about sexual harassment, sexual assault, domestic violence, and other forms of violence against women—as well as harmful myths about poor women and women of color—radical changes in knowledge and attitudes have taken place within the last thirty years. But attitudes about families, marriage, sex, gender roles, power differences, poverty, and other cultural issues don't change rapidly without resistance. Social change takes place slowly, especially when complex historical values and attitudes—such as those about race and gender—are involved. Historians have documented that times of major change are often followed by resistance to that change and attempts to restore a previous status quo. The kinds of confrontational tactics and one-dimensional

Backlashes

backlash (n): a sudden violent backward movement or reaction
—Merriam-Webster's Collegiate Dictionary

According to Susan Faludi, a backlash is not an organized movement or a conspiracy. People are often unaware of their roles in it. But taken as a whole, as she explains in *Backlash: The Undeclared War Against American Women*, the cumulative message of films, media commentary, frivolous lawsuits, and so forth "move overwhelmingly to try to push women back into their 'acceptable' roles. It succeeds to the degree that it appears *not* to be political, that it appears not to be a struggle at all."

As the twentieth century ended, Faludi writes, *Time* declared that women's fight for equality had "largely been won." The message was that feminists had succeeded, that the seriousness of violence against women had been acknowledged, and that to be fair we must now consider men's equality and men's concerns about being treated unfairly by women. While this is a reasonable concern, this argument is also used in a backlash against policies that have been developed to protect women from male violence, as seen in the following examples.

In 1991, social welfare professor Neil Gilbert criticized "radical feminist efforts to impose new norms governing intimacy between the sexes" and "to imply that dating men is a dangerous affair." He claimed that large numbers in acquaintance and date rape statistics are exaggerated because "advocacy researchers" come up with far greater numbers than are reported to law enforcement or college campus authorities. "Radical feminists have distorted the definition of rape and created a bogus epidemic," he wrote, objecting to federal government spending on campus sexual assault prevention programs. A debate ensued between Gilbert and prolific sexual assault researcher Mary Koss, whose landmark 1987 study of rape on college campuses was the target of his criticism. The media extensively covered the conflict between the reality (that sexual assault was far more common than anyone had thought it was before the

1980s) and the backlash reaction of many (that these numbers couldn't be true—if they were, "most men were rapists," or women were falsely accusing many men who were promising college students, ruining their future prospects). This backlash disregarded the impact on the futures of women who had been sexually assaulted while in college, and who could not complete their educations as a result.

Another backlash consists of recent court attempts to undermine laws protecting victims of male violence. In the 2003 rape trial of basketball star Kobe Bryant, defense attorneys tried to have the judge overrule the Colorado rape shield law prohibiting admission of a victim's prior history in court; that case eventually saw intimate details of the alleged victim's sexual history introduced in court and her name and other identifying information released to the public. Terminology recently used in court cases has also reflected a backlash: the Bryant case was notable for being the first in which the term "accuser" replaced "alleged victim." (To be fair to the defendant, the argument for this change goes, the negative implications of the term "victim"—which in all other crimes is what they are called—are intentionally neutralized.) The media's use of the term, along with the recklessly harsh portrayal of the alleged victim's character, resulted in a public "trial by media." In another recent trial, in Nebraska, a woman accusing a man of drugging her at a bar and then raping her was barred by the judge from using the terms "rape," "sexual assault," "victim," "assailant," and "sexual assault kit" in court.

Discrimination lawsuits are another backlash strategy. In 2003, Marc Angelucci, a lawyer and Los Angeles chapter president of the New York–based National Coalition of Free Men, attempted to sue ten Los Angeles-area women's shelters for not allowing men in the shelters. The plaintiff, Eldon Ray Blumhorst, alleged that the women's shelters violated his civil rights by turning him away when he sought shelter as a victim of domestic violence. Uninterested in referrals for shelter offered to him, Blumhorst also didn't seek help from a shelter for men in Los Angeles County. The lawsuit was dismissed as frivolous, but it deeply concerned domestic violence shelter administrators, since many shelters do actually help male victims with counseling and referrals for appropriate shelter.

perspectives required to challenge the hidden status quo are eventually themselves challenged and criticized as too radical or not sufficiently based in reality. Backlashes go to the other extreme, and thinking about issues becomes polarized—as part of change and the resistance to change. Ultimately, a balanced perspective and understanding of the realities of social structural injustices such as gender and racially based violence can take place—but these struggles can go on for years.

As the saying goes, debate is healthy. Feminists who lock themselves into a one-dimensional perspective of what causes violence against women (and how to prevent it) are weakened in advocating for change by the complexity of the issue: there are many exceptions and contradictions to the idea that violence occurs primarily as a result of oppressive gender and patriarchal social structures (for example, the challenge presented by violence in intimate relationships of same-sex couples). Psychologists who are locked into seeing only psychopathology in perpetrators of violence, or in their victims, cannot account for the large numbers of cases in which perpetrators or victims have no identifiable pathology. Those who minimize the realities of violence in women's lives are challenged by the numbers uncovered by research and by the realities of women's situations exposed by advocates and the media. Debate challenges all of us to question our thinking and assumptions and to arrive at more complexity and depth of understanding.

For an example of how debate affects our thinking, let's look at the controversy about defining violence against women and examine how it has stimulated us to seek greater clarity in the ways we describe and label what we see or look for.

How Do We Define Violence Against Women?

The study of violence against women has been filled with conflicts regarding how it has been or should be defined. How violent acts are defined determines whether we see them as frequent or rare incidents, and whether people have a name for the violence that has occurred in their own lives.

What if someone you were dating called you constantly when you hung out with your friends, accused you of having sex with others, and exploded in a rage when unable to reach you, saying that they loved you so much they had to have you with them all the time? If you had never seen anyone behave like this before, you might find it upsetting and try to make this person you cared about feel better. But how soon would you identify this behavior as abusive and controlling, as intimate terrorism, part of a pattern that usually gets worse? If someone you were dating flew into a rage when you were hanging out with friends and hit you as soon as you were alone together, how soon would you identify this as abusive, as intimate terrorism?

Definitions influence what we understand about the causes and effects of violence against women. Definitions are so important that they have been the focus of political, public, and professional debate. The questions researchers and advocates have asked include: should we define the problem broadly, including a wide range of acts that women experience as violent or abusive? Or should we narrow our definition of "violence against women," as happens in the legal system, so that we can easily identify and study the subject? From whose perspective should violence be defined: the perpetrator's intent or the victim's perception? Who or what is being violated? Are the differences among women and the contexts of their experiences represented in definitions? Should definitions identify specific acts or consequences and injuries?

Another of the many questions to consider is whether our understanding of violence against women improves when we separate different acts into discrete categories, or whether they are more realistically seen together since they so often occur together. For example, many women who are physically abused by partners are also raped, and women who are raped by strangers or acquaintances are also physically assaulted. Sexual harassment may consist of a number of acts, such as coercion, verbal abuse, and rape. Dividing them and studying them as separate categories is more convenient for researchers, but doing so doesn't reflect the realities of the culture of violence within which many women live or work. Journalist, author, and critic Ann Jones explains in *Next Time She'll Be Dead: Battering and How to Stop It* how types of violence interweave:

> *What the batterer does inside the family, the rapist and pimp and murderer do outside the family. What the incestuous father does inside the family, the child molester does outside the family. . . . Batterers rape and rapists batter. Many women suffer male violence sequentially at the hands of various men: the girl beaten or sexually abused by her father, stepfather, or older brother runs away only to be picked up by a pimp, raped and battered, and turned into prostitution from which she may try to escape by marrying a batterer if she is not first murdered on the job.*

Definitions influence what is counted by whom, and what we know about how widespread violence actually is. For example, the criminal justice system focuses on perpetrators and illegal incidents of violence, so it counts cases in terms of numbers of reports and numbers of perpetrators. Its documentation doesn't keep track of the number of victims or the number of times one victim is raped or assaulted by the same person. The nationwide crime information maintained by the FBI is valuable in providing a specific picture of the crimes against women that result in arrest and prosecution, but it doesn't show us the bigger picture of violence against women in the United States.

Another way that definitions influence what we know about how prevalent violence against women is has to do with how terms are defined when studies are conducted. If studies ask questions that contain the words "battered" or "rape," they assume that people surveyed all have the same way of defining these terms, or that respondents actually use these terms to label their own experiences. However, this is usually not true. Several studies have reported that the majority of women do not label their experiences with forced, unwanted sexual intercourse as rape. Therefore, studies that ask directly, "Have you been raped?" result in low estimates of rape's prevalence. Meanwhile, studies that use descriptions with several elements ("Have you had sex when you have been forced, threatened, or unable to consent?") rather than single-word terms result in higher estimates.

Similarly, when the definition of violence is limited to physical or sexual assault, estimates of its prevalence naturally are much lower than when the definition incorporates sexual coercion, threats of violence, and economic, verbal, and emotional abuse. Highly influential domestic violence researchers Murray Straus and Richard Gelles define violence broadly, including a range of physically aggressive acts (including shoving, beating, and sexual assault). Their definitions have been used in many subsequent studies and incorporated in domestic violence laws. Gelles, Straus, and others favor identifying intimate relationship violence only by specific behaviors and/or the resulting injuries. However, their definitions are seen as both too broad (since they include fights) and too narrow (since they limit their definition to physical violence) by other researchers, such as Evan Stark, who focuses on coercive control as a significant element in defining relationship violence against women; these critics say that such narrow defining parameters exclude most of the strategies abusive men use to entrap women in their daily lives.

To illustrate the difficulties in defining, and therefore measuring, violence against women, Stark asks his students each year to determine the size of the problem of intimate partner violence and whether it is increasing or decreasing. They search all kinds of sources for the information, take raw numbers, and come to conclusions. "But their self-assuredness dissolves," Stark writes, "when other students muster an equally impressive array of sources to support the opposite conclusion." Violence researchers Maureen McHugh, Nichole Livingston, and Amy Ford present a good analogy of the issue: "We are like the proverbial blind persons stationed around an elephant trying to understand the phenomenon by focusing on different parts," they write. "While one investigates the tail, another claims that the ears or the tusks are the identifying characteristics. Where we are standing impacts how and what we understand about the elephant."

Debates about how violence against women should be defined

most frequently focus on whether broad or narrow definitions are more accurate and therefore more useful. Narrow definitions focus on physical or sexual assault to define violence, often referring to consequences such as injury as a means to determine if violence against a woman has taken place. Legal penal code definitions of the crimes of rape and domestic assault are examples of narrow definitions. They are used in surveys done by government agencies, and they result in much lower estimates of the incidence and prevalence of violence against women than do studies that use broader definitions.

People who believe that narrow definitions are more accurate have several reasons for thinking this. Surveys based on crime reports have to use narrow legal terms because crime data count only illegal acts, such as rape or assault and battery. Because they are so clearly defined by law, legal definitions are often seen as the best way for multiple disciplines (such as police officers, judges, researchers, and educators) to speak the same language. Narrow definitions may increase clarity about a specific form of violence; Richard Gelles argues that when too long a list of abusive behaviors is included in the definition of violence, it "muddies the waters" and makes it impossible to determine causes of or interventions for violence. Narrow definitions make violence easier for researchers to measure and compare across studies, and they can be used across national boundaries and disciplines.

The drawback, say critics, is that these definitions don't reflect women's actual experiences. Few studies using narrow definitions look at psychological, verbal, or economic abuse, forms of violence that are debilitating to large numbers of women. Narrow definitions are also too restrictive to include a spectrum of controlling, coercive, intimidating, and aggressive behaviors that are used simultaneously and are qualitatively different from physically or sexually violent acts. Narrow definitions don't include the context of the violence; for example, it is often said that "a man's slap is different from a woman's slap," yet narrow definitions don't differentiate among the various contexts in which a slap occurs, ignoring differences in gender, age, power, situation, and motivation. Physical and sexual assaults, even the less severe forms, are more brutal when perpetrated in the context of emotional abuse. Many studies that use narrow definitions overlook the nature of the relationship between the victim and the perpetrator, yet studies that use broad definitions find that the nature of the relationship is one of the most important factors and predictors of violence against women.

Rhonda Hammer, a feminist research scholar at the University of California, Los Angeles, and the author of *Antifeminism and Family Terrorism: A Critical Feminist Perspective,* issues a powerful critique against research that decontextualizes domestic violence. "[D]ubious 'empirical' studies that minimize violence against women have the unfortunate effect of dehumanizing and desensitizing the grisly reality of battery and abuse," she writes, "hence, neutralizing and negating the gravity of the problem."

People who criticize the use of narrow definitions generally prefer broad definitions because they view violence against women as multidimensional in nature, consisting of a broad range of violent and abusive actions. There aren't universally accepted broad definitions; in one example, researchers Walter DeKeseredy and Linda MacLeod suggest broadly defining woman abuse as "the misuse of power by a husband, intimate partner (whether male or female), ex-husband, or ex-partner . . . resulting in [the woman's] loss of dignity, control, and safety as well as a feeling of powerlessness and entrapment." Their definition of abuse includes "repeated physical, psychological, economic, sexual, verbal, and/or spiritual abuse"; it also incorporates making "persistent threats or forcing women to witness violence" against others. Another example of a broad definition was used by the 1998 National Violence Against Women Survey (U.S.); that definition included stalking, physical violence, sexual assault, and emotionally abusive and controlling behaviors.

Broad definitions of violence uncover more victimization by including aggressive acts that are considered to be part of the experience of violence yet not included in criminal codes (such as pressuring a woman to have sex or being verbally aggressive); they count incidents and ongoing multiple forms of violence that are not reported to government agencies, inquiring about what women actually experience as abusive and violent. During the last twenty years, definitions and terminology based on survivors' experiences, perspectives, and language have been developed, and this has given women a language and understanding to recognize violence in their lives, empowering them to talk about their own experiences with greater clarity and legitimacy.

Critics of broad definitions believe that since there is no universally accepted broad definition, and definitions differ across studies and through time, the results of studies that use them are inconsistent and not useful to measure real change. Feminists who have problems with broad definitions argue that including acts and situations that are not clearly abusive or violent, and that can be perceived differently by different people, trivializes the serious abuse. Lisa Price, a feminist researcher who analyzes violence, abuse, and gender relations, writes, "I am inclined to favor [a] restrictive . . . definition of violence for the simple reason that a term limitlessly expanded becomes meaningless. Psychological abuse is a form of mistreatment. But in the absence of the exercise of physical force, I hesitate to call these harms and violations *violence.*" Other feminists say that when large numbers of women indicate that they have been victimized—some by being manipulated or coerced to participate in unwanted acts, others by being beaten and forced—then almost all women have been victims, an inaccurate and unacceptable view of women. They are concerned that labeling too many behaviors as violent might result in a breakdown of social exchanges between people, and cause mistrust in relationships, if they too often label each other's behaviors abusive or violent.

On the other side of the fence, political conservatives who are critical of the use of broad definitions see them as designed to inflate the rates of victimization for political and ideological reasons. They believe that these definitions are used to inappropriately influence policies and government spending. Feminists who believe in the accuracy of broad definitions see the challenge by conservatives as evidence of a backlash against the alarming numbers of women who in reality have experienced male violence, viewing the conservative argument as an effort to return to the "status quo" perspective that male violence, especially by white men, is rare, an attitude that is oppressive to women. They believe that successes in advocating for social and policy changes, and in raising public awareness about the realities of violence experienced by women, have triggered a backlash determined to discredit women's experiences and diminish women's power.

In 2005, Maureen McHugh, Nichole Livingston, and Amy Ford wrote an article addressing a postmodern feminist approach to the search for knowledge about violence against women, arguing for more careful consideration of the ways researchers develop their studies and how they conceptualize violence, abuse, aggression, race, and gender. According to postmodern feminists, these concepts are socially constructed—meaning they are not scientific (with only one measurable definition) and they exist only as ideas or categories created by people who are influenced by history, culture, social norms, and, at times, personal or political agendas. The methods that are used to search for information, and the conclusions that are derived from studies, often support some perspectives and minimize others. McHugh and her coauthors argue that intimate violence cannot be accurately characterized in terms of single truths or reductive "either/or" debates; if we can see all forms of violence against women as complex—with multiple dimensions and patterns, dynamic and changing, and interwoven with other aspects of people's lives and relationships—then our knowledge deepens to reflect fuller realities of human experience. The larger contexts in which violence takes place are important to our understanding of its meaning and how it is actually experienced and perpetrated. It is frustrating to accept that violence cannot easily be defined, its causes not easily identified, and to accept that remedies that work for some are oppressive to others—because accepting this means acknowledging that stopping violence is complex, multidimensional, and difficult to achieve.

Are Women as Violent as Men in Relationships?

This has been a "hot" question for thirty years and continues to be argued with a great deal of passion. It is not a question generally asked about other forms of violence seen to primarily involve men victimizing women, such as rape or forced prostitution. Women participate in inflicting violence against other women—for example, women are sometimes perpetrators of human trafficking, and women perform female genital cutting—but questions about the differences between men's and women's use of violence generally focus on violence in intimate relationships.

Maureen McHugh, Nichole Livingston, and Amy Ford's intelligent discussion of these issues in a special 2005 issue of the *Psychology of Women Quarterly* states the problem.

> The "discovery" of new forms and perpetrators of relationship violence challenges many of our theoretical explanations for intimate partner violence. Theoretical explanations that focus on the characteristics or psychopathology of individuals are not sufficient to explain the documented prevalence. Models that cite the institution of marriage do not explain dating violence. Explaining violence in relation to male domination and female subordination does not adequately explain lesbian and gay male intimate violence. Research documenting women's use of violence in their dating, committed, and marital relationships requires us to rethink our understanding of both the reasons for intimate partner violence and our conceptualizations of gender. It is crucial to progress toward more evolved and complex models of interpersonal violence that explain the literature . . . and other data that documents the violence of women. Societal responses to violence . . . depend upon our understanding of intimate partner violence.

Why are there differences of opinion about whether or not women are as violent as men in relationships? There isn't a single explanation, but there are several components to the debate.

While a significant number of studies have shown that women use violence as frequently as men, study results vary with the definitions and methodologies used. Studies of family conflicts involving aggressive behavior find equal rates of assaults by women and men. Crime studies find much higher rates of assaults by men. Open-ended interviews with women who use domestic violence services reveal patterns of coercive control and repeated, chronic violence by men toward their intimate partners. Community and college surveys find more equal use of violence by men and women.

Studies that show that women are equally as violent as men use methodologies and measures such as Murray Straus's Conflict Tactics Scale (see sidebar) that ask about whether specific aggressive behaviors have been used, but that don't include any context for the behavior and don't consider the severity, outcomes, motivation of the perpetrator, or circumstances in which it occurred. These studies don't distinguish between people's motivations for aggression; they don't account for the difference between pushing in self-defense and pushing or hitting to dominate and control. They also ask about the use of aggressive

Conflict Tactics Scales

In 1979, violence researcher Murray Straus developed the Conflict Tactics Scale (CTS), a then-groundbreaking measure of interpersonal interaction that listed fourteen types of behavior occurring in conflict situations (for example, "slapping and hitting" and "discussing the issue calmly"). The original Conflict Tactics Scale included a "Violence" scale, a "Verbal Aggression" scale, and a "Reasoning" scale; users could respond using a scale that ranged from zero ("never") to five ("more than once a month"). In 1996, Straus and his colleagues created an expanded version of the scale, the Conflict Tactics Scale 2 (CTS2), for couples to evaluate victimization. CTS2 mentions psychological and sexual abuse, and it uses the gender-neutral term "partner" rather than "he" or "she."

behavior to handle conflicts, reflecting an inaccurate assumption that conflict is the cause of violence in relationships.

Men's and women's self-reporting of the use of aggressive behavior in a relationship differs between genders. Some researchers have found that women more openly report their own violence, judging it to be more serious a problem than men's judgments of their own violence. Other researchers have found that men more openly report their use of physical abuse. These findings reflect sex role stereotypes that consider male violence to be more excusable or normal and female violence to be more notable and problematic; one effect of this is that men may upgrade women's use of violence, and women may discount or underestimate the violent behavior of male partners.

Less debated is the fact that the consequences of men's and women's violence differ significantly. Men's violence toward female partners more frequently results in injuries, and women receive more severe injuries than do men. Fear of men's violence is a pervasive experience for women, whereas men generally do not fear women. There is a significant difference in the social environment in which relationship violence occurs and the economic, social, and emotional impact of male violence on women. Therefore, many think that gender difference is significant because of the more serious threat, and therefore fear, of male violence for women. Others believe that injury can't be used to determine the difference between women and men, because the majority of assaults committed by both women and men don't cause injuries.

The debate about gender symmetry (the term often used to describe the equal use of violence by men and women) often centers on differences between men's and women's reasons for using aggressive behavior to explain why some studies show that equal numbers of women and men are violent. Those who believe in gender symmetry believe that motivations for violence are the same regardless of gender, and those who don't believe in gender symmetry believe that there are significant differences between men's and women's motivations.

Studies that show equal use of violence often don't ask about the triggers, motivations, or reasons that respondents use violence. From this perspective, violent responses to abuse or violence committed in self-defense cannot be differentiated from angry explosions of violence or violence that aims to control a partner. Without this information, some researchers have interpreted study results to indicate a high prevalence of "mutual combat" in relationships—couples who use violent behavior equally in their fights—and a low prevalence of unilateral abuse of women by male partners. People who believe that women and men have the same motivations for their violence cite as evidence instances in which women who have murdered their husbands have had prior arrest records. They also cite the 1985 National Family Violence Survey (which used the Conflict Tactics Scale) results, which estimated that 25 percent of women's violence was not self-defense, because they were the only ones in the couple to have used violence in the previous year. Therapists and prosecutors have dealt with cases in which women use violence against a male intimate partner for the same reasons that men are violent toward women—for example, to vent rage or to control their partner.

However, studies that investigate motivations for violence have shown that women are more likely to assault a partner in self-defense or in reaction or retaliation to a violent partner, and men are more likely to assault a partner to get their way, explode with anger, or control a partner by intimidating her. In 1994, the first national survey of dating violence among Canadian college students allowed respondents to estimate the extent to which their use of violence occurred as self-defense or fighting back or was initiated by the respondent. The survey participants were asked directly about motivation, and they used a continuum to indicate the degree to which these motivations played a part in the violence. The researchers found that a substantial amount of the total violence used by women was in self-defense, and they were able to reject the mutual combat theory on empirical rather than simply ideological grounds.

The context of the relationship is an important aspect of intimate partner violence. Other aspects of abuse besides the use of violence make a difference in the impact of the violence itself. One example is that when studies survey only currently cohabiting couples, violence committed by former partners is excluded. Men are the aggressors in more than 90 percent of assaults involving former spouses. To understand the impact of the emotional context of violence, think about this: if a person becomes extremely angry and says, "I'll kill you!" and lifts a fist, his partner's reaction will vary depending on what has come before. Even if the threatening person doesn't follow through with the assault, if he has tried to kill his partner before or has constantly undermined her sense of safety in many different ways, the intense fear of actually being killed might trigger violent behavior. The role of coercive control as a motive and as an outcome is important in understanding gender differences in the nature of similar acts. As author Ann Jones states, "Family violence is *not* just a series of isolated blow-ups, the result of anger or stress or too much to drink, though it often looks that way to the woman who is its target. Rather, family violence is a *process of deliberate intimidation intended to coerce the victim to do the will of the victimizer.*"

Patterns of coercive control and psychological abuse may also differentiate the effects of types of violence on victims' psychological well-being as well as behavior. Identifying a variety of patterns and types of violence in intimate relationships may help to explain the conflicting data about gender symmetry. The more gender-equal violence found in community surveys may fit into the pattern of situational couple violence, or aggressive behavior that occurs in evenly matched fights between partners. The more commonly male-perpetrated (and often more severe) violence that is found in clinical samples may fit the intimate terrorism pattern.

Advocate and counselor Alyce LaViolette describes a continuum of four types of patterns in aggressive behavior in relationships. In addition to situational couple aggression and intimate terrorism, LaViolette includes aggression consistently initiated by one partner in conflict situations (but in which the other partner is not frightened or controlled and may even respond aggressively), and psychologically abusive behavior, perhaps in the beginning stages of intimate terrorism, that doesn't terrorize or cause injuries but does undermine and victimize partners. Other researchers have proposed similar breakdowns based on the severity and frequency of aggressive behavior in a relationship. One longitudinal study suggested that those who experience high levels of violence from a partner initially fight back but then give up.

A factor that has been missing in this debate is the diversity of women and men in terms of cultural, ethnic, and religious influences on the use of violence, and the interactions of gender and ethnicity (or intersectionality). Values and norms about men's and women's aggression vary tremendously from one community to another. Researcher and author Gail Wyatt describes her reaction to her study's finding that more than 50 percent of white women surveyed claimed to have been sexually harassed, while only one-third of black women made the same claim: "One possible interpretation is that [harassment] simply occurs more among whites than among blacks. But I think there's more to it than that. Black women may be devaluing their own feelings about the effects that harassment has on them. . . . They may feel that because stereotypes about their sexual availability are so commonplace, there would be little support even if they came forth. The fact that black women tend not to report . . . is [another] indication that they have internalized society's devaluation of them as sexual objects."

The political and ideological aspects of the debate about gender have polarized one view (that women and men are equally violent and use violence for the same reasons) against another (that violence against women by men is far more prevalent, reflecting 90 percent of the instances of intimate partner violence). Why has this debate been so emotional? What is at stake?

Critics of feminist perspectives argue that women's claims as victims of male violence are deliberate misrepresentations based on selecting research results and considering only issues that fit feminist ideology. Researchers such as Murray Straus and Richard Gelles believe that, unlike feminists, their efforts are objective and without bias or emotional investment in a particular outcome. Their research has had strong institutional backing of academia and the National Institute of

Mental Health. It has had a powerful influence on legislators, other policy makers, and subsequent generations of researchers. Their framework for seeing abuse and violence as problems of families in conflict has neutralized the ideological perspectives of the battered women's movement.

Meanwhile, feminist researchers and advocates are alarmed at efforts to depict women as being as violent as men when overwhelming numbers of women are regularly abused and injured by men. According to Rhonda Hammer, in the heat of the controversy, *Ms.* editor Kristen Golden wrote that "much quoted 'experts'" were "claiming that women are as much to blame [for violence] as men: women 'provoke' the beatings—there's that old sick refrain. And the newest twist on equality: women are beating men just as often. How do they figure that? By relying on devices like the 'Conflict Tactics Scale' . . . which measures family violence; attacks are weighted by severity, but the results are generally reported as though a slap on the wrist by a woman is the same as a kick in the head by a man."

Ann Jones continues this argument: "Ever since [Straus and Gelles's work appeared throughout the popular media], pro-feminist academic researchers have engaged themselves year after year in doggedly deconstructing the shoddy studies based on . . . the Conflict Tactics Scale. Their research [and hundreds of other studies since that use variations of the same scale] continues to mislead the public and policy makers alike and to mask the real nature and severity of male violence against women."

Jones quotes respected domestic violence researchers R. Emerson Dobash and Russell P. Dobash: "In Britain, Europe, Canada, Australia, Asia, Africa, and South and Latin America . . . the problem is believed to be and research findings show it to be *violence against women*. . . . One must ask if there is something peculiar about society in the U.S."

After thirty years of efforts to call public attention to men's violence as a hidden and common danger and tragedy in women's lives, a great deal is at stake. Men's violence has been recognized from multiple points of view (for example, health, social justice, and government) as being rooted in social systems and social power dynamics rather than being only a psychological, family conflict, or criminal problem. The struggle for social change to address women's rights and improve their socioeconomic status, and thereby reduce their vulnerability to male violence, has had an impact: as these changes become accepted and institutionalized, they challenge what Evan Stark calls the "normative foundation of male privilege." He comments on the paradox: "Because women are more equal than ever before, men intent on subordinating them have expanded their tactical repertoire beyond coercion, relying heavily on the huge gap that still separates women's formal status as men's equals from their reality." For example, feminist researchers and advocates are worried about a current backlash by "men's rights" and "fathers' rights" groups who are challenging women's right to custody of children in family courts by claiming that women are more violent than men. Meanwhile, researchers have adopted models of family behavior and measures of violence based on assumptions about the family that overlook a well-researched *fact* that gender norms and gendered relations of power are involved in all social relations, and that they are pervasive in the whole social context in which everyone lives. Interviews with men who batter women, for example, show that men believe they are justified in their use of violence, especially when their wives or girlfriends don't conform to the ideal of a "good wife."

In spite of the hostility of the backlash and the gains that are at stake, many feminists have acknowledged the reality of women's violence. They are exploring the differences between men's and women's use of violence as well as the similarities, emphasizing the importance of gender and racial inequality in historical and deeply rooted social structures in understanding both men's and women's violence. Feminist research psychologists Irene Frieze, Maureen McHugh, and others have analyzed the social sciences research on gender and intimate partner violence, deconstructing the polarities of the debate about gender. Feminists bell hooks, Ann Jones, Susan Schechter, and others have objected to the view of battered women as helpless victims, understanding this as a modern version of focusing on women as the source of the problem and leading to extensive research on battered women's personalities, histories, and "poor self-esteem." Linda Mills, a feminist legal scholar, social worker, and onetime victim of domestic violence, wrote a controversial 1999 *Harvard Law Review* article, "Killing Her Softly: Intimate Abuse and the Violence of State Intervention." In a 2002 speech, she challenged "mainstream feminists" and the criminal justice system. She said she would never have reported the violence she experienced to the police: "Doing so would have robbed me of the little dignity I had left. The system patronizes victims by failing to listen to them, usurping their decision-making power and underestimating them—underestimating their ability to negotiate their own safety and underestimating their role in the abusive relationship. Domestic violence is construed as one-sided aggression, when often there is a warped dynamic of intimacy in which both the men and the women are players. It is dishonest to stifle conversation about the ways in which women, too, are aggressive and violent."

The participants in this debate are researchers searching for objective "truths" about observable, measurable phenomena; activists who see gender and race as powerful, socially constructed aspects of social relations, and who believe that no "truth" can be discovered without accounting for them; and postmodern feminists and others who acknowledge that women use violence more frequently than has been previously known but use violence differently than men because of the social context of power differences and social norms. All of these perspectives are debated in a sociopolitical environment in which these "truths" have become the basis for hostile interchanges in a battle over women's rights and the pervasiveness of men's control over and entitlement to women's bodies.

Controversies and debates about issues that stimulate passionate reactions are a natural consequence of significant social change. Institutionalization of changes promoted and fought for by activists is evidence of remarkable success in a relatively short time. Now that law enforcement, legal, medical, mental health, and social service organizations in the United States have made significant changes in their policies and practices to more effectively address violence against women, many people think that the struggle has changed, and that we must only continue to improve and sustain the good work—focusing on addressing safety in public and in private, helping survivors recover, and helping perpetrators stop their violent behavior.

On the other hand, the numbers haven't changed—while crime rates in the United States have gone down, the rates of sexual harassment, rape, and domestic violence have not. Hotlines and other programs receive just as many, if not more, calls for help. Attitudes and erroneous beliefs about violence have been changing, but they change far more slowly than the policies and practices of agencies. The successes have triggered one backlash after another, so the struggle to sustain public awareness of women's rights issues and maintain the gains made is as intense as ever. The conservative sociopolitical climate has undermined the successes of the past thirty years, and many believe that the struggle must be renewed, with more emphasis on ending the societal tolerance for violence against women, more emphasis on guaranteeing women's rights, and less emphasis on services and laws. While the goals have changed, and the focus on changing attitudes and helping people has been successful, institutionalized sexism and racism continue to keep men and women from having equal relationships, access to socioeconomic resources, and political power.

T-shirts hanging on the Mall in Washington, DC, on Saturday, April 8, 1995. The shirts were created for the Clothesline Project, a collaborative installation in which women affected by violence create artwork to express their feelings and bear witness to the issue.
© The Associated Press/Mark Wilson

CHAPTER 5

ACTIVISM

THIS BOOK HAS HIGHLIGHTED THE COMPLEXITY and multidimensionality of the realities and causes of male violence against women. Many different factors contribute to this violence, and efforts to prevent, remedy, and eradicate it must effectively address them, while acknowledging cultural, regional, and other differences as well.

A multitude of approaches are useful in working to eradicate violence against women. Some strategies address the psychological reasons certain men rape, assault, or abuse women (group therapy for behavior problems, for example, in men and boys who have already been aggressive or violent, or who show signs of the potential to become violent in the future). Other approaches involve improving criminal justice responses so that perpetrators are arrested and jailed or mandated to counseling.

Others address the family and interpersonal influences on an individual's behavior, supporting and strengthening families and communities to reduce their exposure to violence and the stress factors that contribute to it. Children who have witnessed and been traumatized by violence—abuse of one parent by another, for example, or violence in their communities—are at risk for using aggressive or violent behavior themselves as they get older. Effective interventions help children and youth recover from trauma, giving them opportunities, activities, and supportive mentors so that they develop self-respect and learn to relate to others in healthy ways.

Strategies to address the health consequences of violence against women use a public health approach: identifying warning signs and risk factors, educating the public to recognize the signs and seek help, educating health providers to improve early identification, and instituting treatment protocols that match what is known about how best to help victims, survivors, and perpetrators. You may have seen public health campaigns on billboards, in televised public service announcements, and on websites, as well as in educational programs that reach students in schools and the public in small groups, forums, and health fairs.

Responsive, competent, and accessible services for victimized individuals and families help support people's emotional, physical, and economic recovery from past violence. They can also prevent future violence—in women's lives and in the next generation. A wide range of services (law enforcement, medical, mental health, and social) deal with problems related to violence against women, and each survivor may seek help from a number of them. For example, it is common for a woman who has been sexually assaulted to call the police, go to a hospital emergency room, receive follow-up medical care in a doctor's office or clinic, and contact a rape crisis center for counseling, information, and advocacy in court; she may also visit a mental health clinic to seek help dealing with the aftermath. Shelters for women fleeing violent relationships, trafficking situations, or slavery have been crucial in diminishing these kinds of ongoing, repeated violence.

These psychological, criminal justice, family support, and public education strategies interface with one another, so that helping individuals and educating the public also contribute to social change. For example, in the 1980s, every time a rape crisis center advocate accompanied a woman who had been sexually assaulted to the hospital, doctors, nurses, and police officers taking reports were made aware of their attitudes about rape, language, and respect for the woman and her rights. When attitudes and beliefs are challenged, more people recognize hidden problems and services can improve, which in turn broadens perspectives of the realities of the problem, contributing to more awareness and changes in attitudes and beliefs.

However, while violence against women is being taken more seriously as a crime, it is still an enormous and pervasive problem. A majority of perpetrators go unpunished. Batterer and sex offender treatment and mandatory domestic violence arrest policies have been effective in many cases, but recidivism is still high. Women don't leave violent relationships if they don't have the means for economic independence. Safety from violence and protection from sexual exploitation are not available to women with very limited options for economic survival. Although it is essential that individual victims receive respectful and competent treatment by all agencies involved, such treatment doesn't stop the violence from occurring in the first place.

All of the approaches described above are extremely valuable and important, and not one of them by itself can adequately change the remarkable worldwide pervasiveness and social tolerance of violence against women. To actually prevent violence against women, social institutions and erroneous historical attitudes toward women must be changed—the goal of social change movements.

The movements to end violence against women have combined political activism with concrete strategies for improving circumstances for women affected by male violence, based on analyses of social structural factors that make women vulnerable.

The emphasis of this chapter is on strategies for social change based on current feminist perspectives, and on the tools used by social movements and advocates to challenge socially accepted norms that endanger women.

Social Change Strategies

Myra Marx Ferree, who studies women's movements, writes that feminism focuses on "access to economic resources, power to effect decisions in the community as a whole, and autonomy in relation to personal life choices." The aim of feminism is "changing gender relations," she explains, "empower[ing] women and . . . chang[ing] social arrangements that unequally benefit men." The many forms of violence against women are rooted in hierarchical power structures that justify and tolerate violence against certain people because they are seen to be innately inferior, and these beliefs are institutionalized in social systems, such as the historical patriarchal domination of the family and male-dominated environments that perpetuate a "rape culture"—in other words, a culture that blames victims and excuses men's sexual aggression because "boys will be boys."

To eradicate violence against women, strategies for change must challenge the status quo of gendered social structures (in, for example, athletics and families), institutionalized sexism and racism, and their intersections with poverty, fundamentalist religious beliefs that restrict women, and discrimination based on sexual orientation. Women are assaulted by men for many reasons: because they are lesbians, because they work in predominantly male environments, or because poverty leads them to unsafe work and living conditions. Women are assaulted by men because they are women.

The vision that drives movements to end violence against women is of a richly diverse world of women who are free to move around without fear in their cities, communities, and homes, and to participate side by side, with mutual respect, with men in all aspects of their political, social, economic, religious, cultural, public, and personal lives. Can you imagine such a vision of your own?

Activism focuses on social change. It consists of political actions and encompasses all kinds of collective efforts to change power relationships at all levels, from interpersonal to international. As political scientists Sarah Henderson and Alana Jeydel explain it in their overview of women's global politics, *Participation and Protest: Women and Politics in a Global World*, social movements are groups of people with a common interest who work together either to change government policies or to change how society perceives something. Women's movements involve the work of women motivated *as women* to work on issues, such as violence, that they view as particularly important; participants are mobilized collectively, as social and political actors. Defining a women's movement can be difficult and challenging: women's organizations represent diverse interests, ideologies, and goals, altered by competing class, ethnic, religious, cultural, and racial identities. Not all women's activism is feminist in orientation. The wide range of women's activism in the world reflects the variety of ways that women define their issues across regions and contexts.

Many of the issues around which women mobilize, though, are common across cultures. Women want to be seen as human beings, not as property. They want fair employment opportunities and the right to be safe from violence in private and in public.

Activists target institutions and social systems for change, and an important strategy for confronting systems that affect women's safety from violence is advocacy. An advocate is someone who speaks, writes, or argues in favor of someone else in public. The tactic of speaking out was an empowerment strategy of the early women's movements to end violence; advocates were women who had been raped or assaulted and women who joined them to fight for a paradigm shift in institutional responses to women.

There are two forms of advocacy: individual case advocacy and systems (or institutional) advocacy. Individual case advocates help individual women obtain what they want and need from local agencies or entire institutions. They aim to help women realize they are not alone in their experiences of abuse or violence, lend emotional and legal support, and accompany women or otherwise help improve their experiences with criminal justice, medical, and welfare systems. In the process, the advocates pressure these systems to be more responsive and not victim blaming and to hold perpetrators of violence accountable.

Individual case advocacy is effective because violence against women affects so many that helping one woman ultimately contributes to changes in these systems. Advocates can simultaneously intervene with individuals and the system. Advocates treat women's responses as normal reactions to their experiences, and working together is an empowering peer support strategy.

Systems advocates work with many cases representing a group of victims and pressure systems to change practices that are unfair or harmful. The primary aim of this form of advocacy is for women to be safe. For example, in the United States in the 1970s and 1980s, state penal codes that defined rape, sexual assault, and domestic assault were analyzed and challenged by antirape and anti–domestic violence activists because they were so rarely enforced, and because they reflected gender bias and social attitudes that endangered women (for example, women had to prove they had resisted rape by showing injuries). Legal advocates in these movements publicized the laws' problems, proposed revisions, and lobbied legislators. With the groundswell of changing public opinion, they succeeded in making major changes in penal codes to clarify perpetrators' responsibility for violent acts. New laws made sentencing more severe, and revised definitions to dispel myths and reflect the realities of sexual and domestic assault.

Similar efforts in other countries whose governments did not recognize violence against women have resulted in the creation of laws against domestic violence, human trafficking, female genital cutting, and honor killings. Enforcement of new laws takes place slowly, as cultural norms that support the violence are more difficult to change than the laws. In Japan (where domestic violence was, until the late 1990s, for the most part not addressed by society and the government), a law was passed in 2001 that defined domestic violence as a crime and created a structure for women to obtain restraining orders from the courts for protection. However, the procedure for obtaining these orders was so complicated and inaccessible that women not only didn't use them for safety, but they continued to believe that they had no right to make their private problems public. Japanese activists continue to work to improve women's access to safety and to campaign for changes in social norms regarding men's right to dominate their families and punish their wives.

Other systems that have been targeted for change are schools and workplaces, environments in which unequal power makes women vulnerable to sexual harassment. Although U.S. public policy established in

Muslim Women Organizing for Human Rights: Pinar Ilkkaracan

"The first time I had a rebellious feeling was with my parents, when I was trying to get that freedom at fifteen," activist Pinar Ilkkaracan says. "But it wasn't until my twenties that I began realizing that it wasn't my parents; it was the larger society. It's the patriarchy that affects women around the world irrespective of their class or education, and that was the point at which I decided to change things."

Through consciousness-raising groups, Ilkkaracan realized that just being a woman made one a potential target of violence all over the world. Consciousness-raising approaches are central in the training programs she has developed; she sees them as the best tool for change. According to Linda Basch, president of the National Council for Research on Women (U.S.), Ilkkaracan has played an important "role in demystifying cultural taboos and misconceptions about customary violent practices against women—practices that have often been portrayed incorrectly as uniquely Islamic by the news media and by certain political groups."

Ilkkaracan is the founder of Women for Women's Human Rights—New Ways (WWHR), a Turkish organization that advocates and lobbies for women's human rights nationally, regionally, and internationally, conducts women's human rights training programs, and coordinates the international Coalition for Sexual and Bodily Rights in Muslim Societies (CSBR), the first solidarity network in Muslim countries, working with thirty-eight groups in Algeria, Egypt, Jordan, Lebanon, Morocco, Palestine, Tunisia, Turkey, Yemen, Bangladesh, Indonesia, Malaysia, Pakistan, and the Philippines.

Ilkkaracan's work has significantly improved the treatment of women under Turkish law. Her efforts have led to laws allowing battered women to secure protection orders and recognizing women as equal partners in marriage. In 2004, her efforts succeeded in reforming the Turkish penal code to "protect women's sexual and bodily autonomy," which included measures criminalizing marital rape and sexual harassment in the workplace.

Ilkkaracan has used a variety of powerful activist strategies. The WWHR and the CSBR have formed pressure groups that organize action campaigns using print and broadcast media. They publish their research and views and engage with policy makers in creating and implementing legislative changes. They are actively involved in formulating international resolutions and treaties.

1964 that sex discrimination in workplaces and schools was illegal, it wasn't until legal advocates worked with sexual harassment victims in the 1980s to sue government agencies and businesses for violating their civil rights that women and girls' safety at work and in school was actually addressed. When huge costs were incurred as a result of these suits, employers and educational institutions began to proactively change policies and institute procedures for preventing and responding to sexual harassment.

Poverty contributes to women's vulnerability to violence, at times keeping women in violent relationships or forcing them to work in sexually exploitive conditions. Advocates have worked to improve systems that provide financial support for women and their children. Individual case advocates support women as they apply for financial assistance, working with a rigid bureaucratic system to bend rules to keep women safe. For example, local welfare departments have had practices making it easy for batterers to get access to recipients' information, revealing abused women's whereabouts when they were in hiding or in a shelter. Advocates and survivors at first succeeded in getting welfare departments to change these rules for individual women's safety and then to change and institutionalize those policies for all survivors. Meanwhile, welfare system advocacy at federal and state levels has led to changes in welfare laws; policies and programs have been redesigned to provide specialized services for victims of abuse and to allow women abused by partners more flexibility and time to overcome obstacles to employment resulting from violence.

Sometimes the momentum for change is stimulated by a tragedy or a high-profile case that saturates the media. The public debate over Anita Hill's allegations against Supreme Court nominee Clarence Thomas in 1991 created an environment for advocates to successfully pressure government agencies, businesses, and other institutions to enact clear policies and procedures regarding sexual harassment. In 1994, the trial of football star O. J. Simpson for the murder of his ex-wife Nicole Simpson revealed Simpson's history of spousal abuse, spurring discussions about the realities of domestic violence and the failure of police and other systems to prevent the murder. (While this case received excessive public attention, it was also clear that there were hundreds of other similar cases in which women were repeatedly threatened and abused, and some murdered, that never received any attention at all.) Simpson was acquitted, but the trial's publicity caused the domestic violence movement's advocacy efforts to be recognized on a larger scale; as a result, more public funding was dedicated to preventing intimate partner violence and supporting survivors. Later, in 2004, the trial of Scott Peterson for the murder of his pregnant wife, Laci, prompted antiviolence experts to call for increased attention to women's high risk of relationship violence during pregnancy.

Changes and new priorities in the economic and political climate of the United States can sometimes create momentum in exposing and addressing violence against women. When George W. Bush was lobbying Congress to endorse the invasion of Afghanistan in 2001, the media were saturated with stories about the mistreatment of women by the Taliban, the fundamentalist Sunni Muslim movement that ruled Afghanistan at the time. The United States and international public learned of Afghan women being prohibited from working or attending school after the age of eight, being forced to cover their entire bodies in public at all times, and being beaten or worse for violating the strict religious dictates of sharia law. In response, Congress legislated funding specifically earmarked for programs in Afghanistan for education and support of women and girls. When the media reported, in the 1990s, that hundreds of women and girls were sexually assaulted in ethnic cleansing and genocidal violence in Bosnia and in Rwanda, worldwide attention to the long-hidden reality of the rape of civilian women and girls as part of war led to outrage and advocacy to punish military and government leaders for war crimes. Reports of rape during previous wars, such as the Vietnam War, surfaced. International laws were changed as a result; for example, the International Tribunals on the former Yugoslavia and Rwanda led to the establishment of the International Criminal Court. These historical moments spawn movements, or they expand the numbers of people interested and motivated to participate in existing movements.

U.S. Movements to End Violence Against Women

The history of social change efforts to stop violence against women has involved different movements, often working together. Most people involved in the movements to end violence against women in the United States would agree that the forms of violence overlap, coexist, and in actuality can't be separated from one another because of their common roots and manifestations. There are a great many overlapping areas of activism this book could cover, but this section will limit its focus to the recent histories of two major U.S. activist movements: the movement to end sexual assault and sexual harassment and the movement to end domestic violence.

The Clothesline Project

The Clothesline Project, a participatory violence-awareness art installation, was started in 1990 by a coalition of women's groups on Cape Cod, Massachusetts. In it, women "air their dirty laundry" and demonstrate the extent of violence against women by creating shirts that represent victimization and survival. Women affected by violence express their emotions through artwork on the shirts; the decorated shirts are then hung on a clothesline in a public place, where they can be viewed by others to "witness" the problem of violence against women. Doing the laundry has historically been (and is often still) considered women's work, and in the days of close-knit neighborhoods women often exchanged information over backyard fences while hanging their clothes out to dry. On college campuses, weeklong displays of the shirts end with Take Back the Night marches.

Coverage in several national magazines has created a tremendous national response and transformed the Clothesline Project from a single, local, grassroots effort into a national campaign. There are an estimated five hundred projects nationally and internationally, in forty-one states and five countries, involving an estimated fifty thousand to sixty thousand shirts. This grassroots network continues to grow, in local cities and as far away as Tanzania.

The Antirape Movement

The antirape movement started in the United States in the early 1970s as an outgrowth of the women's movement. In consciousness-raising discussion groups that took place all over the country, women spoke about the many ramifications of being female in their families, homes, workplaces, schools, and in public. Many in the women's movement were daughters of women who had become self-sufficient, moved to cities, and been part of the war effort in World War II. They had witnessed their mothers' transformation resulting from the postwar propaganda of the 1950s that encouraged women to return home from their wartime work, asserting that paid employment must be the arena of men, and that women who work rather than putting all of their efforts into mothering would produce damaged children. White women and women of color who had to work because survival took two incomes, or because there wasn't another parent to share the financial burden—in other words, women whose survival depended on their paid labor—were judged as inadequate as women and parents. And many of the women who had thrived from their participation in the public arena during the war felt frustrated and unfairly confined by being relegated to home and family. These new social norms resulted from a combination of an economy with more limited jobs and the psychological and social impact of Freudian ideas about the essential role of mothers for early childhood development and the idealization of women's fulfillment in their roles as mothers rather than in work outside the home.

The 1960s and 1970s were a time of rapid social change; the civil rights and anti–Vietnam War movements mobilized the entire country in a clash of values regarding how social systems and governmental decision making disempowered and disenfranchised the majority of people in the United States. Women activists in these movements gradually became enraged (as the nineteenth-century women's suffrage movement members had before them) by their second-class roles in relation to activist men.

With this historical background, young white women of the 1970s challenged their mothers' roles in the postwar 1950s and their own roles in a social environment that was rapidly changing public and private lives. Young women of color were conflicted because the new women's movement often did not address issues that concerned them—justice regarding economics and employment was an issue for men of color as well as women, and alliances with men to change this were crucial. Their struggles regarding their roles as women were completely different, especially their historical struggles with white women who supported abolition of slavery and equal rights for women but not equality among women of all races.

The dialogues among women in the late 1960s and early 1970s inevitably turned to the hidden subject of sexual violence. Even among women, this was a taboo subject. Many women had been silent for years about having been raped, assaulted, or harassed by strangers, coworkers, employers, dates, or acquaintances. Discussions about violence inflicted by husbands emerged more slowly. Many women had restricted themselves to private lives because of their unspoken fear of the danger that lurked for them in public without the protection of men. Many women harshly judged, blamed, and ostracized women who had been raped, categorizing them as "other," "not like me." Many women of color had protected the men of color in their lives from further oppression by racist systems by keeping silent about their experiences with sexual violence, viewing women who reported rape as betraying their communities. In effect, women had been isolated from one another, which came to be seen as a means of maintaining a patriarchal social structure in which women are dependent on and subordinated to men—as well as being men's caretakers and silent protectors.

When women began to speak among themselves about hidden sexual violence, they became enraged and frightened, and they determined to do something about it. In a pattern of events similar to those that occurred in other cities in the early 1970s, a friend of one of the activists involved with a local women's center in Los Angeles had been raped, and the police had not taken it seriously. A group of women protested the lack of police response, put up posters, and spoke publicly about the rapist, who lived in the community. What followed shocked everyone in the women's center: the phone started ringing relentlessly. Women called with their stories, questions, and concerns about sexual violence—some were coping with recent rapes, and others wanted to talk about rapes that had happened many years before. They talked about painful experiences of loneliness and guilt, and of confidence in themselves and relationships destroyed. Schedules were arranged so that the phone could be answered and callers would have someone to talk to. A public forum (then called a speak-out) was planned, and hundreds of women attended, stimulating a powerful surge of action and the launching of a volunteer hotline. The women from the women's center—now called the Anti-Rape Squad—coordinated volunteer schedules and education and gathered donations to cover the phone bill. Women organized all kinds of efforts to speak and write publicly about sexual violence and to protest the ways in which women were revictimized in the course of making police reports. Volunteers accompanied women and girls to hospitals, police stations, and courts to advocate for respectful treatment.

With a feminist understanding of sexual violence, and a commitment to help victims and change society, the social movement to stop rape grew rapidly throughout the United States. The Anti-Rape Squad, which became the Los Angeles Commission on Assaults Against Women (now Peace over Violence), was organized as a feminist collective, with shared power and decision making, as were the majority of grassroots, volunteer-based rape crisis centers. The survivor-empowering model of advocacy and counseling developed by the centers emphasized the victim's need to maintain control over decisions that affected her. Victims decided whether to report the rape and who to tell about the experience. Taking their cue from the women's movement's emphasis on peer support, center workers treated women who had been raped as the experts, mistrusting professionals (such as therapists, police officers, and doctors) who had historically blamed women for rape. The centers all had (and still have) similar programs: twenty-four-hour volunteer-run hotlines providing information, referrals, and crisis counseling;

medical and legal advocacy and accompaniment; peer support groups for survivors; public education; training of professionals; and political actions such as protests and legislative lobbying for stronger laws that are not biased against women.

An example of the international momentum of the antirape movement can be found in Take Back the Night marches, which have become large annual collaborative protests in cities and on college campuses all over the United States. The marches grew out of a 1976 meeting of the International Tribunal on Crimes Against Women held in Brussels, Belgium. Women from all over the world came to give testimonials about incidents in which they had been victimized simply because they were female. After the meeting, women marched through the city with candles; at an open microphone, participants spoke about their experiences. The first Take Back the Night march in the United States was organized in San Francisco, California, on November 4, 1978, by Women Against Violence in Pornography and Media; women marched with candles through the red-light district to protest rape and pornography. Three thousand demonstrators took part in the march and speak-out. Subsequent marches received tremendous attention from the public and grew larger each year, each one attended by thousands of women.

In the years that followed, rape crisis centers sought public funding from government agencies to pay staff to keep up with the growing demands of their work. Public funding led to the centers' reorganization as nonprofit service agencies with administrative staff and boards of directors. Some rape crisis centers moved away from their political and social movement origins to be eligible for government funding. Others affiliated themselves with mainstream organizations such as YWCAs and district attorneys' offices in order to fiscally survive. Although many rape crisis centers became more like social service agencies than groups of activists, the women working in them have continued to engage in political action, lobbying, and social change efforts. They continue to engage large numbers of volunteers, many of them survivors, who provide peer counseling and support for women in crisis. They have

Take Back the Night

Andrea Dworkin, a lifelong activist and a radical feminist author known for her strident critiques of pornography, spoke the following words in a speech given at the 1978 Take Back the Night march in San Francisco. Her call to action, which appears in Laura Lederer's anthology *Take Back the Night: Women on Pornography*, still resonates as a powerful demand, highlighting the persisting need for women to work together to claim the right to be safe and confident on their own streets.

Tonight we are going to walk together, all of us, to take back the night, as women have in other cities all over the world, because in every sense none of us can walk alone. Every woman walking alone is a target . . . Only by walking together can we walk at all with any sense of safety, dignity or freedom. Tonight walking together we will claim to the rapists and pornographers and woman batterers that their days are numbered and our time has come. . . . Tonight, with every breath and every step, we must commit ourselves to going the distance: to transforming the earth on which we walk from prison and tomb into our rightful and joyous home. This we must do and this we will do, for our own sakes and for the sake of every woman who has ever lived.

organized powerful state and national networks. They continue to be responsible for many of the social, legal, and institutional changes that benefit women who have been sexually assaulted and contribute to public awareness to prevent sexual assault and sexual harassment. They have been recognized as leaders and experts, and they have participated in and advised government and private policy planning commissions and councils.

The antirape movement has had an enormous impact on many aspects of society in the United States. Once hidden and unspoken, every aspect of women's experiences with sexual assault has been publicly addressed. Federal, state, and local public funding has been dedicated to research, policy changes, and services. Even our language around the issue has changed: terms such as "date rape," "acquaintance rape," "marital rape," and "sexual harassment" are known and used by all kinds of people, not just researchers or experts. Media treatment of sexual assault, while still often stereotyped, is far more realistic than it was thirty years ago. Romanticized scenes of women being overtaken by strong men, such as Rhett Butler carrying Scarlett O'Hara up the stairs in *Gone with the Wind,* are less common than scenes such as Sarah Tobias's brutal gang rape and its aftermath in *The Accused,* which in 1988 marked a turning point in the depiction of rape in films. The realities about the effects and aftermath of sexual assault on victims and those close to them are now recognized and taken seriously by the media, courts, service providers, and family members and friends. Medical, legal, social, educational, and employment systems have significantly changed their policies and practices surrounding sexual assault. None of this would have occurred without a powerful social movement of sexual assault survivors and a climate of social change.

The movement's strategies for changing laws and criminalizing violence against women were effective. New rape laws clarified that a woman did not have to be injured to prove that she did not consent to sex. Women's sexual histories were made inadmissible in rape trials, prohibited by rape shield laws, blocking a defense often used by rapists in court to intimidate victims and justify rape as inconsequential if the woman had been sexually active before the rape (a prevailing myth). This addressed a serious obstacle for women who formerly would not report rape to law enforcement because they knew they would be attacked, blamed, and humiliated by police and defense attorneys. (Although this kind of mistreatment still occurs, and women continue to be reluctant to report sexual assault, the criminal justice system has greatly improved, and the reporting rates have increased: formerly estimated at one in ten, it is now estimated that one in four victims report sexual assault to police.) Laws were passed allowing charges of rape to be brought in circumstances in which a woman is unable to give consent (for example, if alcohol or drugs interfere with her awareness of what is happening, if she is mentally or developmentally disabled, or if she has been deceived—and the rapist knowingly has sex without consent). Another myth—that married woman cannot be raped by their husbands—was dispelled by penal codes making marital rape a crime. These changes represented a paradigm shift in which the realities of rape became visible, women's stories were more likely to be believed, and rape by people known to the victim as well as by strangers was dealt with seriously.

Another arena in which women's antiviolence activism has made enormous progress is medicine. Sexual assault victims visit hospital emergency rooms for treatment for injuries, to prevent pregnancy and sexually transmitted diseases, and to allow police to collect evidence for prosecution. In the early years of the antirape movement, victims complained of insensitive treatment by hospital personnel: interviews in public spaces, cold, clinical examinations, and crude comments by medical professionals, which were often experienced as a second rape. Women spoke up about sloppy or neglected evidence collection and inadequate preparation for prosecution. The centers pressured hospitals and state and county health departments to improve their rape response systems, which resulted in the establishment of sexual assault response team (SART) programs. The first of these collaborative teams of specially trained sexual assault nurse examiners, rape crisis center advocates, police, and prosecutors was developed in 1976 in Tennessee. The number has grown, and the programs still operate nationwide. SART teams use a standardized protocol to provide treatment of injuries, emergency treatment for STDs and pregnancy, and crisis intervention (advocacy and counseling), and they collect medical-legal evidence that is reliable in court.

The Battered Women's Movement

It has become well known—by survivors; by their friends and families; by communities all over the United States; and by religious leaders, politicians, police, prosecutors, and judges—that intimate partner violence happens to hundreds of women every day. They are often trapped by social attitudes, poverty, fear, and trauma. But there are remedies and resources for safety that didn't exist just a relatively short time ago.

Before 1970, most women who were assaulted by their husbands could find safety only with families and friends or in shelters for alcoholics, disaster victims, or homeless people. Most of the time, they were blamed for the violence. Haven House, an emergency shelter for wives and children of violent alcoholic men, was founded in Pasadena, California, in 1964 by an AlAnon group. In 1971, the director of Haven House at the time, Ruth Slaughter, realized that there was more to the patterns of repeated violence she was witnessing than alcoholism. She was approached in 1975 by researchers, community activists, and rape crisis center advocates who wanted to learn how to support women who were speaking out about their experiences with violence at the hands of husbands and boyfriends. Women whose assailants were the men they lived with were in complicated situations, and social attitudes about them made it difficult for them to be listened to and supported by those who hadn't been through the experience themselves. Slaughter described her experience. "None of us had the answers. We knew nothing except that women like myself—African American, Latina, and white—came to Haven House needing safety. I started with the stories of the women, and wrote proposals for funding, and met with others, joining together to learn. I didn't see myself as a feminist. I was an ordinary African American housewife with a job. The needs of the women were so great; I had to work with women who had the same passion as I had to end this violence. We all changed." She couldn't answer the questions then, but she joined with feminists, community activists, and formerly battered women to define the problem of what they later called *domestic violence* (and what some called *domestic terrorism)*, and she became a national leader in the multicultural movement to stop violence against women in their homes.

In the momentum of changing political consciousness and activist organizing, abuse of women by their husbands and boyfriends was suddenly seen, like rape, as another manifestation of men's right to control women in our society. Even more hidden than rape by the privacy of the home and family—and seen as resulting from women's "masochism" and failures in relationships or by men's alcoholism—societal and professional attitudes about intimate partner violence were intolerant ("Why is she still there if she doesn't somehow like it?"), dismissive (Jackie Gleason's joke about punching his nagging wife "right to the moon" always got a big laugh), and filled with victim blame ("She must do something to get him that mad!"). According to legal advocate Ellen Pence, who developed model domestic violence programs in Duluth, Minnesota, "Women were devastated by the personal betrayal of their abusers but perhaps equally harmed by seemingly endless ways that police officers, clergy, welfare workers, judges, family members, landlords, attorneys and therapists found to blame them for their partners' violence. Advocates heard the same stories in every state. Of course, every story had its parochial twist, but the overarching theme of community collusion with batterers was starkly visible."

At women's movement conferences and meetings (such as the 1977 International Women's Year Conference in Houston), women who had been in battering relationships met one another and spoke out. A national battered women's movement began to grow. During the same time, when rape crisis center hotline volunteers received calls from women whose rapists were their husbands or boyfriends, many didn't know how to respond and their judgmental attitudes alienated callers. Some advocates saw these sexual assault experiences as having the same roots as acquaintance or stranger rape, and they sought information about how to be helpful; others believed that women choose violent intimate partners and that as a result their problems were very different from those of other rape victims. These differences led some antirape movement organizations to expand to incorporate strategies to end relationship abuse, but others separated themselves from the battered women's movement, and in some cities, the two movements developed completely separately.

Susan Schechter, an activist and movement leader who documented the history of the movement, described its beginnings in her groundbreaking book *Women and Male Violence: The Visions and Struggles of the Battered Women's Movement.* "By claiming that what happened between men and women in the privacy of their home was deeply political, the women's liberation movement set the stage for the battered women's movement," she wrote. "Domination was uncovered operating not only in the public political world, but also in the private political sphere of the family." The importance of this message was that women were not to be blamed for their husbands' unhappiness, and that women had rights as autonomous human beings.

Some advocates in the battered women's movement were feminists, but the majority were not. They had a broad spectrum of reasons for their strong personal commitments, and many didn't agree about marriage and women's roles. But they all agreed that women needed to be safe, and that contrary to public attitudes and the movies, large numbers of women were not safe in their own families.

Between women's speaking out and seeking help, and new research efforts, a picture of alarming numbers of women abused in their homes emerged—and this was early on when "abuse" was defined as physical violence, when less was known about the spectrum of violent behavior that actually occurred, and when large numbers of women continued not to report violence or seek help.

Unlike the hotline responses to sexual assault, which were possible to implement with a cadre of volunteers and a telephone, finding safety for women who had to flee their homes wasn't simple. A woman who needs emergency housing is usually running from immediate danger from a husband or boyfriend, or from a female partner, who has beaten her and is threatening more violence. They seek shelter as a last resort and for two basic reasons: they don't have another safe place to go, and they must hide where they can't be found because their lives are in danger.

To offer safe places for women and their children to hide in the midst of a violent attack, formerly battered women and women who had seen violence in their families as children responded to hotline callers by sheltering women in their own homes. Other groups of survivors and advocates organized within their neighborhoods and communities and obtained donations of funds or property to establish safe spaces to shelter abused women and their children. Some shelters opened in unused city-owned buildings or in spaces offered by organizations such as YWCAs. Most of the original shelters were in large old houses, able to house ten to fifteen women and children at a time. Eventually many of the shelters were able to move into larger buildings designed for communal living and their other services.

Each shelter operated a twenty-four-hour hotline offering callers safety planning, information, referrals, peer counseling, accompaniment to police and hospitals, and access to emergency shelter. The shelters provided safe housing at secret locations and about thirty days of counseling and advocacy to help women plan their next steps. Women shared childcare and household duties, and they shared rooms because space was limited—sometimes struggling to get along with one another and usually giving one another emotional support.

Women using shelter services were often from the communities in which the shelters were situated and so found that the people in the shelter environment were also from their own communities. However, many immigrant women and women of color needing these crisis services found that their particular needs weren't met in programs where staff and volunteers didn't speak their language or were so unfamiliar with their cultural backgrounds that they weren't helpful. Some experienced discrimination by other residents, volunteers, and/ or staff members. In large, multiethnic cities such as Boston, San Francisco, and Los Angeles, women of color established domestic violence shelters with culturally specific services. Multilingual shelters for Asian women and Spanish-speaking shelters for Mexican and South and Central American women also assisted women with issues related to their immigration status. Shelters for African American women addressed the scarcity of services, discrimination in the systems they needed access to, alliances with churches, and other advocacy issues specific to local communities. In Los Angeles by the mid-1990s, shelters for African immigrants, Moslem women, and Jewish women had been established.

As domestic violence programs grew, they provided advocacy with the welfare system, access to job placement or training, health assessments for the women and their children, supports for nonviolent parenting, and childcare, activities, and counseling for children. Networks of shelters organized and referred to one another to move women safely out of their own neighborhoods and to find alternative emergency housing when their own shelters were full. Shelter programs also provided legal advocacy, counseling and drop-in support groups for women who were not in their shelters, public education, and professional training. They lobbied for better laws and advocated for better systemwide responses by police, judges, hospitals, doctors, mental health professionals, and social service agencies (welfare and child protective services).

According to Susan Schechter, by 1982, estimates were that between three hundred and seven hundred safe home and shelter projects had been started in the United States. (Between 1998 and 2007, the number passed two thousand.) As soon as shelters opened their doors, they were unable to house the numbers of women seeking refuge. Schechter cites a 1977 survey of 163 programs revealing that 11,710 women and 14,473 children had been sheltered by then, with a total of 46,838 women receiving residential and nonresidential services. A 1979 Minnesota survey showed that 70 percent of women requesting emergency housing were turned away because shelters were full.

When they leave, women who have found refuge in the crisis shelters often stay with friends or family, sometimes moving to another city to do so safely. Others are able to find housing and reestablish themselves, usually moving to new communities to be safe. Others return to the homes they have fled, some with changed circumstances, and others hopeful that the abuse will stop. It has been estimated that about 50 percent of women leaving shelters return to their previous lives, stronger after the respite they had in the shelter but not permanently free from violence. Many women continue to maintain contact with the shelters for support after they leave, attending support groups and meeting with or telephoning their advocates.

As programs grew, it became clear that there was a need for transitional housing for women who were no longer in crisis, but who needed time and resources to establish themselves independently rather than returning to violent relationships. Therefore, many shelter programs today also have transitional housing programs that help survivors and their children make the transition to more permanent residences, paying a small percentage of their income for rent so that they can save enough for first and last month's rent in a new place of their own. These programs include other support services, such as counseling and help to find jobs and housing.

The battered women's movement has also worked to promote a wider range of options through which a perpetrator of violence can get help. An important fact recognized by women's advocates is that while women who have been abused in relationships are often misdiagnosed (and seen as "crazy"), men who abuse women in relationships may appear more mentally healthy and functional because they have *not* been the target of repeated severe violence. This knowledge has been the foundation of standardized psychoeducational groups for batterers based on a model developed by Ellen Pence of the Duluth Domestic Abuse Intervention Project in Minnesota. These groups have provided impetus to change for abusers and rapists who twenty years ago would have faced no consequences or treatment for their violent behavior. Standards for intervention set by many states now include education regarding the unacceptability of sexist and demeaning attitudes toward women, as well as tools for stopping aggressive behavior.

After safe shelter, legal reform was a priority of the movement. Laws in the United States against intimate partner abuse didn't exist before 1970, and victim-blaming attitudes prevailed throughout the criminal justice system. The battered women's movement made remarkable changes in the legal systems that abused women often encounter. In some cities, lawsuits against police departments for endangering women because of their lack of response led to laws and enforcement policies to improve police intervention. As a result of legal reform since 1977, domestic violence has been clearly defined by law. Police officers can make arrests in misdemeanor domestic violence cases without having witnessed the assault, previously required for misdemeanor arrests. Prosecutors can proceed with a trial using other evidence (such as police photos of injuries) if the victim does not want to be a witness because she is afraid or trying to protect her partner. Police can make criminal arrests to protect abused women who are being harassed and threatened, but who haven't yet been victims of violent acts, by enforcing civil protection orders. In some states medical practitioners are required to report cases of domestic violence to law enforcement, a measure aimed at overcoming a historical lack of response by hospitals and clinics when women seek help for injuries sustained during an assault.

After a 1984 pilot project in Minneapolis showed that mandatory arrest was a deterrent to further violence by a partner, every state adopted mandatory arrest laws. Based on years of police officers not arresting violent husbands and boyfriends they sympathized with, these laws require police to make an arrest when called to a domestic violence scene and not use their own discretion. Later replication of the first study showed that mandatory arrest is effective as a deterrent in only some cases, when the perpetrator is afraid of being arrested because he has something serious to lose, such as a job or community respect. In other cases, arrest doesn't keep the perpetrator from being violent again, and in still other cases arrests actually lead to more violence.

The most significant legal innovation developed by the movement is domestic violence civil protection and temporary restraining orders. In 1976, the Pennsylvania Coalition Against Domestic Violence was the first advocacy organization to approach a state to adopt civil restraining order legislation (the Protection from Abuse Act) to provide a civil remedy for abuse victims. By 1994, all fifty states had adopted some form of domestic violence protection order. These laws established the broadest definitions of domestic violence and allowed judges to write orders that fit the realities of each woman's situation. This was historically significant: it was the first time that women were able to obtain protection from the state from relationship violence. Restraining orders continue to be the primary form of protection for victims of domestic violence. They are immediately available, issued by a judge in a civil, not criminal, proceeding. The victim describes the nature of the situation, and the judge issues the order when there is "reasonable proof of a past act or acts of abuse." The judge orders the violent partner not to attack, assault, threaten, harass, or call the victim and may also include other provisions, including orders to keep away from the victim's residence or work and awarding the victim temporary custody of children. The primary goal of civil restraining orders is preventing further physical abuse (which is what victims often want the most), not punishing batterers. Women who are financially dependent upon their violent partners suffer more when criminal prosecution and prison lead to the loss of their only source of income—and imprisonment of abusers does not necessarily prevent future violence. The actual effectiveness of restraining orders to keep violent partners away varies with the abusing partner's circumstances and motivation, but they are effective steps in empowering survivors to protect themselves and can make it possible for them and their children to stay in their homes.

Beyond safety, the battered women's movement has actively developed innovative approaches to preventing violence. The movement created a sea change in attitudes and norms about violence in the private sphere of intimate relationships. While many people still puzzle over "why women stay," large numbers of people know that the real question is "Why do men beat and torment the women they love?" Recent advocacy to prevent violence has focused attention on interventions and changing socially supported attitudes of potentially violent men: Esta Soler, director of the Family Violence Prevention Fund for twenty-six years, has been breaking new ground with "Coaching Boys into Men" and "Founding Fathers" campaigns that invite men to teach boys that violence against women and children is always wrong.

Men's groups have participated in the movements to end violence against women, actively working to change men's attitudes and social norms. Groups such as Men Stopping Violence (an independent organization of women and men who conduct programs to hold men accountable for violent behavior and advocate for violence prevention nationally and in local communities) and other organizations all over the United States, such as the White Ribbon Campaign and Men Against Sexual Violence, are committed to organizing men to sign pledges of awareness and activism to stop violence against women. Some of the organizations teach men "bystander interventions," to intervene in the behavior of men who are likely to commit violence.

Others have focused on the unique circumstances of African American, Hispanic, and other ethnic communities. Formed in 1993, the Institute on Domestic Violence in the African American Community (IDVAAC) in St. Paul, Minnesota, objects to the "one-size-fits-all" approach commonly provided by domestic violence services in mainstream communities, explaining that this approach isn't relevant or effective for African Americans, who disproportionately experience stressors and conditions that lead to violence in their homes. Its Safe Return Initiative reflects an increasing concern about violence stemming from high rates of incarceration in communities of color all over the United States, and it works to keep families safe as ex-offenders are released from prison to decrease the vulnerability of such families to domestic violence.

International and Transnational Activism

The global movement to end violence against women involves the efforts of women's activist organizations in many countries that communicate with one another, and the transnational efforts of women from several countries working together. This section will highlight work within four selected areas of major global significance: international organizing to stop female genital cutting, end sex trafficking, address wartime sexual violence, and promote women's human rights.

Female Genital Cutting

The campaign against female genital cutting has received widespread attention since the 1980s, but it actually began well before then. In the 1960s, the World Health Organization (WHO) announced its opposition to female genital cutting, and in the 1970s the organization initiated efforts to disseminate medical information and encourage elimination of the practice. In 1982, WHO issued a formal statement to the UN Commission on Human Rights, recommending that governments adopt policies to end female genital cutting and educate the public about its harmful effects and encouraging local women's groups to take action. WHO emphasized female genital cutting as a human rights as well as a health issue and generated support from African governments and nongovernmental organizations.

By the 1990s, public opinion against female genital cutting in the United States had evolved from a small effort struggling to get attention to a large movement. In 1993, Representative Patricia Schroeder introduced a ban on female genital cutting, without success; in 1996, Senator Harry Reid added an amendment onto the Illegal Immigration Reform and Immigrant Responsibility Act criminalizing such surgeries on girls under eighteen years old, which passed and was signed into law. The law also required the then–Immigration and Naturalization Service (now U.S. Citizenship and Immigration Services) to provide information on the "severe harm to physical and psychological health" caused by female genital cutting to everyone who is issued immigrant or nonimmigrant visas. By 2000, the INS had produced and distributed information in six languages to overseas embassies in designated countries. Another provision of the 1996 law mandated the Department of Health and Human Services to identify U.S. communities where female genital cutting was likely to be practiced and to design and conduct education programs on the dangers of the practice. This was to be done in collaboration with people from the ethnic groups that practice it and with representatives of organizations that have expertise in preventing it.

Ghanaian activist Efua Dorkenoo, an international campaigner against female genital cutting, established the Foundation for Women's Health Research and Development (FORWARD) in 1983. She was working as a midwife in Ghana, and then in London, when she realized the impact of female genital cutting on African women. She found that it frequently caused complications in childbirth, particularly in women who have had the most severe form, infibulation. Dorkenoo started FORWARD with a group of supporters to promote women's health. Between 1995 and 2001, she was the World Health Organization's expert on female genital cutting, helping the WHO put it on the agendas of the health ministries of countries where it is practiced. She has been influential in passing laws against the practice in England and subsequently in other countries.

With support from the WHO and the United Nations, Dorkenoo conducts an educational program in Africa and in immigrant communities around the world. Her training program sends specialist healthcare workers into communities that practice female genital cutting. She advocates discussing the practice not solely in terms of health consequences but also as a human rights problem, emphasizing that it is carried out mainly to suppress the sexuality of girls and women. She believes strongly that the issue is not only the physical mutilation; it is the message that it gives out and the context in which it happens. In Africa, where the practice is widespread, there is a strong movement to stop it (and all other forms of violence against women).

Giving testimony in Scotland in 2004, Dorkenoo said, "[C]onfronting [female genital cutting] as 'mutilation' is difficult for women, especially initially, because they must question what their parents did to them. They have been told that it was a good thing and that it made them a good woman. . . . In our work with communities, we use the terminology with which people feel comfortable. For example, if they call the practice 'circumcision,' it is important for us to call it circumcision. . . . Gradually, we bring in the human rights dimension until people use the term 'female genital mutilation' without problem, as do many people in Africa."

Legislation making genital surgeries illegal is one tool to deal with the issue. In England, the law provides child protection interventions to prevent it, with penalties for parents who have the operation performed on their children, and support for community groups to undertake education activities, including work with mosques and religious leaders.

The law can be used to assist parents who feel pressure from family elders to submit their daughters to the practice. Sometimes, women or couples have been able to use legislation to enable them to say to family elders, "I would have circumcised my daughter, but I couldn't, because it's illegal here."

A multipronged approach is important: the law can protect children and make the point that it is not acceptable, but communities and women's organizations also play an important role, discouraging the practice through culturally sensitive education and support while helping women and girls who have already undergone genital cutting to get access to healthcare.

A multinational approach is also vital, especially in countries where female genital cutting is widely practiced. The Inter-African Committee on Traditional Practices Affecting the Health of Women and Children (IAC) was started by African women after a 1984 conference in Dakar, Senegal. As of 2000, it had affiliates in most countries where genital cutting is practiced. It is a membership network of twenty-eight African countries and fifteen affiliates in Europe, Canada, Japan, and New Zealand. The organization also has consultative status with the African Union and the UN Economic and Social Council, and official status with WHO. The purpose of the IAC is to promote the basic human rights of women and children by campaigning against this and other harmful traditional practices while promoting beneficial practices. It uses many of the organizing tools of social change movements discussed earlier in this chapter: community mobilization, advocacy, education, and lobbying. In addition, IAC mobilizes resources to improve local women's groups' capacity to conduct educational campaigns in their own communities; the organization sponsors workshops, seminars, training for nurses and midwives, information campaigns, and research and surveys. IAC Ghana reported on its campaign in a Muslim community that practiced female genital cutting. A large assemblage of people was shocked by a drama, performed by schoolgirls, about the complications of the procedure. As a result, the traditional leaders decided to slaughter four cows in a ceremony to pacify the ancestors and gods; afterward, they concluded that the ancestors were ready to accept the change and publicly banned female genital cutting.

IAC educational campaigns have through the years led to the demystification of traditional practices, and its informational campaigns and lobbying have contributed to laws against female genital mutilation in several African countries. There is evidence that the practice is decreasing.

Transnational Organizing on Women's Rights, Trafficking, and Sexual Violence

In the 1970s, development agencies such as the United Nations began to organize international conferences to address women's issues. In 1972, the United Nations declared 1976–1985 as the Decade for Women, and the First World Conference on Women was held in Mexico City in 1975. The United Nations Fourth World Conference on Women, held in Beijing, China, in 1995, was the largest and most influential of all the World Conferences on Women. It was attended by seventeen thousand representatives from 189 countries and territories, the UN organizations and its specialized agencies, as well as government and nongovernmental organizations. In conjunction with the conference, a Nongovernmental Women's Forum was held, attended by 31,549 people.

The Beijing Conference was a turning point in world understanding of women's human rights. Delegates to the conference approved a Platform for Action—far stronger than earlier UN conference platforms—with major advances in the areas of violence against women, health, economic equity, and the rights of girls. It called for the promotion and protection of the universal human rights of women, defined rape as a war crime, and condemned other forms of gender-based violence such as genital mutilation, domestic violence, marital rape, and dowry-related violence. The rights of girls and young women to privacy, confidentiality, and respect were affirmed in language that sought to provide protections for young women in various situations, varying from being sold into sexual slavery to making reproductive health decisions. Individual countries made specific commitments to address violence against women: Austria pledged to grant political asylum to women who had been victims of sexual violence; Belize agreed to pass laws to protect women against sexual harassment; Luxembourg agreed to open a center for young women victims of violence and sexual abuse; Mauritius committed to enacting domestic violence legislation; and the United States pledged to implement a Violence Against Women Act. (The United States did pass the Violence Against Women Act in 1994 and renewed it in 2000 and 2005; it provides funding for programs and research, tightens standards for criminal justice system responses, and allows immigrant women abused by husbands to petition for legal residency.) Islamic countries, meanwhile, failed to win language in the platform allowing a country's religious or cultural practices to supersede the Platform for Action's unequivocal commitment to women's human rights.

According to Sarah Henderson and Alana Jeydel in *Participation and Protest,* these conferences were critical: they brought attention to gender issues and led governments to make changes in their own agencies. They pressured development agencies to recognize the diversity of women's experiences and acknowledge that factors such as class, age, marital status, religion, and ethnicity or race have a significant impact on women's lives and women's issues. The global conferences helped facilitate the emergence of transnational feminist networks in the 1980s and have helped those networks significantly expand and diversify in the years since 1995.

Activist and documentarian Helene Rosenbluth attended women's conferences in Mexico City and Nairobi (in 1975 and 1985, respectively) and was a delegate for the Women's International League for Peace and Freedom in Beijing in 1995. She was amazed by the magnitude of international connections among women at the Beijing Conference and the Nongovernmental Women's Forum. The previous decade's Nairobi Conference was not publicized enough—many women representatives nearby in Africa didn't attend—but women from Africa and all over the world made remarkable efforts to raise the money to get to Beijing. Enthusiasm about the global women's movement was high. A major paradigm shift had taken place in the two years since the World Conference on Human Rights in Vienna in 1993. International human rights organizer Charlotte Bunch had claimed that "women's rights are human rights" and that violence against women was a human rights issue, and the global women's movement now had a cohesive focus. Women worldwide had heard stories from the International Court about genocidal rapes in Bosnia and Herzegovina and stories about women seeking asylum in the United States and Europe to flee from female genital cutting and rape. They came to Beijing to make changes.

The Internet, more widely used than before, facilitated global communication. María Suárez Toro from Costa Rica had started an international radio show via shortwave radio to facilitate communication among women in developing countries who didn't have AM/FM radio or access to the Internet, and at the Beijing conference she offered people Internet access and taught them to use it. Hands-on workshops helped women at Beijing learn to use email, and computer companies donated computers to women's centers in developing countries so that organizers could use the Internet. As Rosenbluth says, "If we had the Internet and no Beijing conference, it wouldn't have happened, and if we had Beijing and no Internet, it wouldn't have happened." The personal international connections made in Beijing intensified commitments to transnational efforts to end violence against women, and they continue today.

Transnational activism to combat sex trafficking has also been mobilized by the international conferences on women's rights. Historically, awareness of sexual and labor exploitation has fluctuated during the past century: international agreements banning human trafficking in the early 1900s were enacted as responses to sensationalized stories of European and American white women being kidnapped and forced into sexual slavery in Africa and the Middle East; no one recognized that non-Western women had been subjected to this for centuries. After a 1949 UN convention on trafficking, the international community was largely silent about trafficking issues, until Kathleen Barry wrote *Female Sexual Slavery* in 1979. Her exposé revealed evidence that trafficking for prostitution was growing, that in some countries high-level officials were directly involved with importing women from developing countries for sexual slavery, and that the international law enforcement agency Interpol was aware of these problems but they were never made public.

The 1976–1985 UN International Decade for Women stimulated global research and activism on trafficking in women. In 1983, Kathleen Barry, Charlotte Bunch, and Shirley Castley organized a Global Feminist Workshop to Organize Against Traffic in Women; thirty-four women from twenty-four industrial and developing countries gathered in Rotterdam. Disagreements between Western and non-Western women about abolition of prostitution versus less drastic solutions, and about Western women's (rather than non-Western women's) administration of a global network, resulted in the conference ending in a stalemate.

The global campaign against trafficking has benefited from international campaigns against violence against women, and it has become an important issue on the international political agenda. Women's antitrafficking organizations have proliferated worldwide, and campaigns to stop sex slavery and sex tourism are now firmly established in Asia and Europe.

Transnational activist organizations pressure governments to enact antitrafficking laws and decriminalize treatment of illegal immigrants who are trafficking victims. They work to empower women to prevent entrapment into slavery. Sex tourism, child sexual exploitation, and militarized prostitution in Asia perpetrated by Europeans and Americans have also been the targets of activists, especially in the Philippines and Thailand. Trafficking is a complex issue; there is no single strategy to combat it. Every activist organization works with other organizations, whether internationally or locally. The Coalition to Abolish Slavery and Trafficking (CAST) began in 1998 as a multidisciplinary group of organizations (including the Thai Community Development Center, the Little Tokyo Service Center, and the Legal Aid Foundation) that had worked together to assist seventy-two Thai women discovered in a sewing sweatshop in a residential area of Los Angeles in 1995; the women had been enslaved there for seven years. End Child Prostitution, Child Pornography and Trafficking of Children for Sexual Purposes (ECPAT), in Bangkok, started in 1990 when researchers at a tourism consultation exposed the degree to which child prostitution was increasing in many Asian countries. After its first International Conference in 1992 (in which children actively participated), ECPAT was established as a group of organizations, and it now has eighty groups in seventy countries as members. It works with organizations in Western Europe, the United States, and Australia—major sending regions for sex tourists—and focuses on laws, monitoring, arrest, and prosecution of child sexual exploitation.

According to Andrea Bertone, a consultant to international organizations that combat trafficking, transnational activism has followed a "boomerang pattern of influence" in which domestic nongovernmental organizations "bypass their inaccessible governments and directly search out international allies, usually [organizations] in Western countries, [to] appeal to their own governments to try to pressure the inaccessible governments. Such networks provide access, leverage, and information to less powerful Third World actors. . . . Few, if any governments sanction trafficking; however, many corrupt government officials are involved directly and indirectly with trafficking. . . . Activism targets changes in this governmental behavior."

Activism to stop sexual violence in armed conflict and in refugee situations has been most effective through transnational efforts to develop and enforce international laws. In 2001, the International Criminal Tribunal for the former Yugoslavia convicted Dragoljub Kunarac, Radomir Kovac, and Zoran Vukovic for rape, torture, and enslavement of women during the conflict in Bosnia. According to Henderson and Jeydel, "These three cases are the first time in history that an international tribunal has brought charges against military leaders solely for crimes of sexual violence against women. And it is the first time that an international tribunal has found rape and enslavement a crime against humanity. This decision is important because it establishes a legal precedent for charging soldiers and combatants who use sexual violence against women during war."

An outcome of this decision was the establishment of the International Criminal Court, created by the Rome Statute in 1998, for the purpose of prosecuting violators of women's human rights.

International organizations such as the United Nations, Amnesty International, and Human Rights Watch monitor, investigate, expose, and denounce wartime sexual violence as a human rights violation. They visit refugee camps and war-torn areas to interview women and document human rights abuses; then they pressure governments to stop the abuses and prosecute the offenders. Their large international memberships collectively influence leaders to pressure governments through education, media exposure, petitions, letters, and calls. Amnesty International declares, "We are calling on governments and armed groups to end impunity for violence against women during times of conflict and post-conflict."

Future Directions

The work to end violence against women has been tremendously successful, but there is a great deal yet to accomplish. As you have been reading each chapter, have you felt outraged about injustices, alarmed by the many obstacles that women face worldwide, and inspired by women's efforts to fight for social justice? Perhaps you have ideas of your own about what you can do to make your own contribution toward ending violence against women. Or maybe you are already involved. Activism starts with one person talking to another. Have you discussed what you have been reading or studying with friends and family members? If so, you have already begun.

Where do movements to end violence against women go from here? They must continue to do what they are doing, and they must continue to grow and develop new strategies to meet new challenges as they arise.

Some of the remedies covered in this book have worked well for some women and communities, but they have unintentionally caused harm to others. Future activism must be directed at finding ways to address the complexities in women's lives and differences among women by modifying overly simplistic legislation and developing other remedies to support existing ones. For example, advocates are finding that arresting an abuser can worsen violence or life circumstances for some battered women; advocacy and other means of finding safety and independence from violent partners must be developed in coordination with the criminal justice system as alternatives.

To ensure safety for survivors, activist Andrea Smith suggests using "base-building approaches" (that is, recruiting people who are not activists to become activists) that define survivors as organizers or potential organizers rather than as victims or clients—strategies that don't depend on the police or other institutions to solve intimate partner violence. She also emphasizes strategies to end violence, not simply to provide services. One of her examples of this kind of strategy is an organization that focuses on base building, Sista II Sista in Brooklyn, New York. This organization of young women of color addresses violence against women in their neighborhoods. They created a video project documenting police harassment after a girl was killed and a second sexually assaulted and killed by police. The group has also created a program, "Sisters Liberated Ground," to organize its members to monitor violence in the community. The program recruits and trains girls to become activists on their own behalf.

Legal advocacy has always been complex, and as changes have been institutionalized—such as referrals to shelters and standardized protocols for respectful treatment of victims and evidence collection—new challenges are created for advocates. For example, in Los Angeles, Peace over Violence advocates who respond to the Los Angeles Rape and Battering Hotline have just been trained and credentialed to accompany immigrant survivors to federal courts to petition for legal residency if they have been abused by and separated from legal resident husbands.

Ellen Pence proposes actions that can return advocacy to focus more on social change than services while still capitalizing on growth of the past thirty years. She proposes building critical reflection and community organizing activities into advocates' work, giving battered women and advocates decision-making control over the work, and strengthening collective advocacy efforts of progressives in the community by linking the antiviolence work of marginalized groups. In addition, she suggests rebuilding programs to minimize dependence on institutions that subjugate women.

Barbara Hart, an activist, legal reformer, and leader in the movement to end domestic violence, has called upon activists to address the invisibility of violence against women of color. "We have not assisted migrant women to organize in their communities," she said at a 1999 conference on ending domestic violence.

> *We have not brokered resources for immigrant women to escape the threat of deportation. We have not been active with the African American church in America to encourage them to seek social justice and safety for women in their fellowships. We have not partnered with Indian women to assure them that non-Indian men who commit violence against women on tribal lands are legally restrained or incapacitated. We have not worked in housing projects with residents to design and implement safety strategies. We have not figured out and implemented translation services for all the women who don't speak or write English. . . . Not enough, not very well.*

In the years since Hart spoke these words, movements for change in these communities have begun, but future activism must expand these efforts.

Jackson Katz, in his 2006 book, *The Macho Paradox: Why Some Men Hurt Women and How All Men Can Help*, writes,

> *It is rare to hear thoughtful discussions about ways that our culture defines "manhood," and about how that definition might be linked to the endless string of stories about husbands*

killing wives, or groups of young men raping girls that we hear about on a regular basis. . . . For the past two decades I've been part of a growing movement of men, in North America and around the world, whose aim is to reduce violence against women by focusing on those aspects of male culture, especially male-peer culture, that provide active or tacit support for some men's abusive behavior. . . . No one should expect rapid results. . . . We need a far-reaching cultural revolution . . . about changing the sexual norms in male culture, from elementary school playgrounds to the common room in retirement communities, and every locker room, pool hall and boardroom in between.

To continue the progress of social change, primary prevention strategies that target men are needed—in addition to, not instead of, outreach to women. New directions to end violence against women must include role models and mentors for boys who exemplify relationships with women based on respect. High school football coach Joe Ehrmann, a former NFL star, challenges his players' ideas about masculinity, asking them, "What kind of son are you? What kind of teammate are you? What kind of friend?" explaining, "Success comes in terms of relationships, empathy, inclusion, and integrity, and having a cause beyond yourself."

"In the end," antiviolence organizer Esta Soler says, "we cannot change society unless we put more men at the table, amplify men's voices in the debate, enlist men to help change social norms on the issue, and convince men to teach their children that violence against women is always wrong."

Rapid changes in technology have expanded the possibilities for reaching women—locally as well as internationally. Activists are using the Internet for organizing, education, communication, and interactive support. The Rape, Abuse and Incest National Network, an organization that operates a national sexual assault hotline, recently added Web-based secure and anonymous live crisis intervention services to reach young women who are more likely to use the Internet than the telephone, and who have been sexually assaulted or are looking for information to prevent sexual assault.

New challenges are ahead, already apparent because of political, economic, and social changes of the early twenty-first century. Conservative governments and powerful religious fundamentalist movements, in the United States and elsewhere, are challenging established human and legal rights, such as freedom of speech, the right to habeas corpus (right to seek relief from illegal detention), and the right to due process (right to the processes of law) in a climate of fear of terrorism. President Bush's 2001 global gag rule denies U.S. family planning assistance to foreign NGOs that use funding from any other source to perform abortions in cases other than a threat to the woman's life, rape, or incest; that provide counseling and referral for abortion; or that lobby to make abortion legal or more available in their country. This has already deprived many women of needed healthcare and increased their vulnerability to poverty and violence. As conflict, war, and refugee situations proliferate, sexual violence is increasing at alarming rates in many countries, including Sierra Leone, Somalia, Democratic Republic of Congo, and Iraq.

Before the U.S. invasion in 2003, women and girls in Iraq had gradually lost rights guaranteed in the Iraqi Provisional Constitution of 1970. In 2001, the UN Special Rapporteur on Violence against Women reported that since 1991, an estimated four thousand women and girls had been victims of honor killings, and men who killed or assaulted a female relative in defense of family honor were now exempt from prosecution and punishment. The 2005 Iraqi Constitution guarantees equal rights for women as long as those rights do not violate sharia, or Koranic law—which does not protect women from violence. Since 2003, journalists have reported instances of Iraqi women and girls being sexually mistreated by American soldiers. Even if not sexually assaulted, Iraqi women who have been detained by American soldiers are seen by their families as having been raped, and they are therefore in danger of being ostracized or murdered by families or villagers. As in most areas of disruption and chaos, and where there is an influx of soldiers, women are forced into prostitution because of poverty, often due to losses of husbands and sons who have been arrested or killed, in a country where women's access to education and employment is restricted. Women's groups in Iraq and transnational organizations are actively addressing these challenges to women's rights and safety; the power of local organizing and transnational connections among women worldwide sustains social movements that promote women's and girls' rights and safety.

To conclude, Barbara Hart's words remind us all to continue these social movements to end violence against women:

> *As we approach a new millennium many of us want to capture the time of social revolution for history. Three expressions arose early in the movement [against domestic violence] and I'd like us to remember them. "Never another battered woman." Another was "Stop rape." . . . The third was "We can all be battered and raped"—an important lesson we in the movement have learned. More than one hundred years ago, Elizabeth Cady Stanton promised, "[We here] solemnly vow that there will never be another season of silence until women have the same rights everywhere on this green earth as men." [African American a cappella group] Sweet Honey in the Rock has more recently proclaimed our sacred vow of struggle for justice—"We who believe in freedom will not rest until it comes."*

READER'S GUIDE

Questions for Discussion

How do you think your family or the people you grew up with would respond to learning that you had been sexually assaulted or abused by someone you were dating? What aspects of your culture or religion would influence how they responded?

What do you consider the most important development in the United States thus far in the struggle to end violence against women? Why?

Name three portrayals of violence against women you've encountered in the media recently. How were these incidents depicted? What social values or ideas do you think these depictions might reflect?

Do you think men's use of violence in relationships is the same as women's or different? Explain your thinking.

Think of a recent time when you've found yourself in an environment in which gender inequality or hostility against women was expressed and/or encouraged. Did you notice at the time that this inequality or hostility was being expressed? What did you do in that situation?

In your own life, consider all the realms (at school, in the workplace, etc.) where a policy against sexual harassment was in effect. How do you think the policies' existence affected your daily experiences in those environments? How do you think it affected others' experiences? How might your time there have differed if those policies were not in place?

Do you think fraternity or campus rape is an example of "rape culture"? Explain your answer.

Ask a group or class to vote: How many of you believe it is better to limit the definition of violence against women to physical/sexual acts that cause injuries? Why? How many of you believe it is better to broaden the definition of violence against women to include verbally, emotionally, and financially abusive and coercive and controlling behavior, as well as violatory physical and sexual acts? Why?

Think of one thing you have been doing or will do after reading this book that will contribute in some, even small, way to stopping or preventing violence against women. What is it?

Topics for Research

Pick one of the following topics and research how the situation in your area has evolved in past decades:

Rape and Sexual Assault

Questions to consider: What sort of legal, medical, counseling, or advocacy resources do rape survivors have in your city? How far away is the nearest rape crisis center, and what services does it offer? Has your city or campus ever hosted a Take Back the Night march or other rape awareness event? What year did your state institute a law against spousal rape?

Sexual Harassment

Questions to consider: How do your state's laws define sexual harassment? When were the first laws against sexual harassment instituted in your state?

Abuse

Questions to consider: What local services exist for abused women and their children? When were they established? What services do they provide? If you cannot find any such organizations in your city, where is the nearest such organization you can find? How much would it cost to travel there from your city?

Assignments

The next time you are shopping, pay attention to the labels and notice where consumer items you buy were made. Do you recognize any of the places that this book has mentioned as a city or country where women have been exploited?

Obtain a copy of your school's, your workplace's, or a major local employer's sexual harassment policy. What does it say?

FURTHER READING AND RESOURCES

TEXTBOOKS

Barnett, Ola W., Cindy Miller-Perrin, and Robin Perrin. *Family Violence Across the Lifespan: An Introduction*. Thousand Oaks, CA: Sage, 2005.

Renzetti, Claire M., Jeffrey L. Edleson, and Raquel Kennedy Bergen. *Sourcebook on Violence Against Women*. Thousand Oaks, CA: Sage, 2001.

Sokoloff, Natalie ed., with Christina Pratt. *Domestic Violence at the Margins: Readings on Race, Class, Gender, and Culture*. Piscataway, NJ: Rutgers University Press, 2005.

READING

Bancroft, Lundy, and Jay G. Silverman. *The Batterer as Parent: Addressing the Impact of Domestic Violence on Family Dynamics*. Thousand Oaks, CA: Sage, 2002.

Bancroft, Lundy. *Why Does He Do That? Inside the Minds of Angry and Controlling Men*. New York: Berkeley, 2002.

Batstone, David. *Not for Sale: The Return of the Global Slave Trade—And How We Can Fight It*. San Francisco: Harper, 2007.

Bertone, Andrea. "Transnational Activism to Combat Trafficking in Persons." *Brown Journal of World Affairs* 10, no. 2, 2004.

Bunch, Charlotte, and Roxanna Carillo. *Gender Violence: A Development and Human Rights Issue*. New Brunswick, NJ: Center for Women's Global Leadership, 1991.

Crenshaw, Kimberlé. "Mapping the Margins: Intersectionality, Identity Politics, and Violence Against Women of Color." *Stanford Law Review* 43, 1991.

Fortune, Marie Marshall. *Sexual Violence: The Unmentionable Sin: An Ethical and Pastoral Perspective*. New York: Pilgrim, 1983.

García-Moreno, Claudia, Henrica A. F. M. Jansen, Mary Ellsberg, Lori Heise, and Charlotte Watts. *WHO Multi-Country Study on Women's Health and Domestic Violence Against Women: Initial Results on Prevalence, Health Outcomes, and Women's Responses*. Geneva: World Health Organization, 2005.

Hammer, Rhonda. *Antifeminism and Family Terrorism: A Critical Feminist Perspective.* Lanham, MD: Rowman and Littlefield, 2002.

Henderson, Sarah, and Alana Jeydel. *Participation and Protest: Women and Politics in a Global World.* New York: Oxford University Press, 2007.

Herman, Judith. *Trauma and Recovery: The Aftermath of Violence—From Domestic Abuse to Political Terror.* New York: Basic Books, 1992.

Johnson, Michael P. "Patriarchal Terrorism and Common Couple Violence: Two Forms of Violence Against Women in U.S. Families." *Journal of Marriage and the Family* 57, 1995.

Johnson, Michael P. "Violence and Abuse in Personal Relationships: Conflict, Terror, and Resistance in Intimate Partnerships." In Anita L. Vangelisti and Daniel Perlman, eds., *The Cambridge Handbook of Personal Relationships.* Cambridge, MA: Cambridge University Press, 2006.

Katz, Jackson. *The Macho Paradox: Why Some Men Hurt Women and How All Men Can Help.* Naperville, IL: Sourcebooks, 2006.

Leventhal, Beth, and Sandra E. Lundy. *Same-Sex Domestic Violence: Strategies for Change.* Thousand Oaks, CA: Sage, 1999.

Levy, Barrie. *In Love and In Danger: A Teen's Guide to Breaking Free of Abusive Relationships.* Berkeley, CA: Seal, 2006.

McHugh, Maureen C., Nichole A. Livingston, and Amy Ford. "A Postmodern Approach to Women's Use of Violence: Developing Multiple and Complex Conceptualizations." *Psychology of Women Quarterly* 29, 2005.

Miles, Al. *Violence in Families: What Every Christian Needs to Know.* Minneapolis, MN: Augsburg Books, 2002.

Price, Lisa. *Feminist Frameworks: Building Theory on Violence Against Women.* Halifax, NS: Fernwood, 2005.

Raymond, Janice G., Jean D'Cunha, Siti Ruhaini Dzuhayatin, H. Patricia Hynes, Zoraida Ramirez Rodriguez, and Aida Santos. *A Comparative Study of Women Trafficked in the Migration Process: Patterns, Profiles and Health Consequences of Sexual Exploitation in Five Countries (Indonesia, the Philippines, Thailand, Venezuela and the United States).* New York: Coalition Against Trafficking in Women, 2002.

Renzetti, Claire M., and Raquel Kennedy Bergen. *Violence Against Women: Readings from 'Social Problems.'* Boulder, CO: Rowman and Littlefield, 2005.

Richie, Beth E. *Compelled to Crime: The Gender Entrapment of Battered Black Women.* New York: Routledge, 1996.

Rozee, Patricia D. "Violence Against Women: Women's Fear of Rape: Causes, Consequences, and Coping." In Joan C. Chrisler, Carla Golden, Patricia D. Rozee, eds., *Lectures on the Psychology of Women.* New York: McGraw-Hill, 2007.

Sanday, Peggy Reeves. *Fraternity Gang Rape: Sex, Brotherhood, and Privilege on Campus.* New York: New York University Press, 1990.

Sanday, Peggy Reeves. *A Woman Scorned: Acquaintance Rape on Trial.* New York: Doubleday, 1996.

Sheffield, Carole. "Sexual Terrorism." In Laura L. O'Toole and Jessica R. Schiffman, eds., *Gender Violence: Interdisciplinary Perspectives*. New York: New York University Press, 1997.

Shell-Duncan, Bettina, and Ylva Hernlund, eds. *Female "Circumcision" in Africa: Culture, Controversy, and Change*. Boulder, CO: Lynne Reinner, 2000.

Stark, Evan. *Coercive Control: How Men Entrap Women in Personal Life*. New York: Oxford University Press, 2007.

Tjaden, Patricia, and Nancy Thoennes. *Stalking in America: Findings from the National Violence Against Women Survey* (NCJ 169592). Washington, DC: U.S. Department of Justice, National Institute of Justice, Centers for Disease Control and Prevention, 1998.

FILMS AND VIDEOS

Broken Vows: Religious Perspectives on Domestic Violence, 1994. Faith Trust Institute: www.faithtrustinstitute.org

Calling the Ghosts: A Story About Rape, War and Women, 1996. Story of Bosnian women, victims who became leaders in establishment of the International Criminal Court. Women Make Movies: www.wmm.com

God Sleeps In Rwanda, 2004. Stories of the leadership of women who survived genocide in Rwanda. Women Make Movies: www.wmm.com

Killing Us Softly 3: Advertising's Image of Women, 2000. Media Education Foundation: www.mediaed.org

Shame, 2007. The rape of Mukhtaran Mai in Pakistan. The Brink: www.brink.com

Sisters and Daughters Betrayed, 1996. Realities of sex trafficking and forced prostitution. Global Fund for Women: www.globalfundforwomen.org

Trading Women, 2003. Sex trafficking. Documentary Educational Resources: www.docued@der.org

WEBSITES

Amnesty International USA's Stop Violence Against Women Campaign: www.amnestyusa.org/stopviolence

Battered Women's Justice Project: www.bwjp.org/menu.htm

Coalition Against Slavery and Trafficking: www.castla.org

Coalition Against Trafficking in Women: www.catwinternational.org

Family Violence Prevention Fund: www.endabuse.org

Human Rights Watch Women's Division: www.hrw.org/women

National Coalition Against Domestic Violence: www.ncadv.org

National Online Resource Center on Violence Against Women: www.vawnet.org

National Sexual Violence Resource Center (NVRC): www.nsvrc.org

Rape, Abuse and Incest National Network (RAINN): www.rainn.org

UN Development Fund for Women: www.undp.org/unifem

SOURCES

Chapter 1

Bem, Sandra Lipsitz. *The Lenses of Gender: Transforming the Debate on Sexual Inequality.* New Haven, CT: Yale University Press, 1993.

Bernstein, Nina, and Leslie Kaufman. "Women Likelier to Be Slain by a Partner than a Stranger." *New York Times,* October 22, 2004.

Brownmiller, Susan. *Against Our Will: Men, Women and Rape.* New York: Simon and Schuster, 1975.

Bunch, Charlotte, and Roxanna Carillo. *Gender Violence: A Development and Human Rights Issue.* New Brunswick, NJ: Center for Women's Global Leadership, 1991.

Collins, Patricia Hill. "The Sexual Politics of Black Womanhood." In Pauline B. Bart and Eileen Geil Moran, eds., *Violence Against Women: The Bloody Footprints.* Thousand Oaks, CA: Sage, 1993.

Crenshaw, Kimberlé. "Mapping the Margins: Intersectionality, Identity Politics, and Violence Against Women of Color," *Stanford Law Review* 43, 1991.

Crenshaw, Kimberlé. "Whose Story Is It, Anyway? Feminist and Antiracist Appropriations of Anita Hill." In Toni Morrison, ed., *Race-ing Justice, En-gendering Power: Essays on Anita Hill, Clarence Thomas, and the Construction of Social Reality.* New York: Pantheon, 1992.

Crenshaw, Kimberlé. *The Intersectionality of Race and Gender Discrimination.* African American Policy Forum, 2000.

Dasgupta, Shamita Das. "Women's Realities: Defining Violence Against Women by Immigration, Race, and Class." In Raquel Kennedy Bergen, ed., *Issues in Intimate Violence.* Thousand Oaks, CA: Sage, 1998.

Davis, Angela Y. *Women, Race and Class.* New York: Random House, 1982.

Deer, Sarah. "Ask Amnesty." Amnesty International USA. www.amnestyusa.org /askamnesty/live/display.php?topic=82.

Dobash, R. Emerson, and Russell P. Dobash, eds. *Rethinking Violence Against Women.* Thousand Oaks, CA: Sage, 1998.

Dutton, Donald. "The Origin and Profile of the Abusive Personality." Conference on Healing and Treating Violence, Anger and Trauma, Las Vegas, NV, October 28, 2004.

Dutton, Donald, and Daniel J. Sonkin, eds. *Intimate Violence: Contemporary Treatment Innovations*. New York: Haworth, 2002.

Ellison v. Brady. 924 F.2d. 872, 9th Circuit, 1991.

Fisher, Bonnie S. *Violence Against Women and Family Violence: Developments in Research, Practice, and Policy*. U.S. Department of Justice: National Institute of Justice, 2002.

Fisher, Bonnie S., Francis T. Cullen, and Michael G. Turner. *The Sexual Victimization of College Women*. Washington, DC: U.S. Department of Justice, Bureau of Justice Statistics and National Institute of Justice, 2000, NCJ 182369.

Fitzgerald, Louise F. *The Last Great Open Secret: The Sexual Harassment of Women in the Workplace and Academia*. Washington, DC: Federation of Behavioral, Psychological and Cognitive Sciences, 1993.

Fortune, Marie M. "Religious Issues and Violence Against Women." In Claire M. Renzetti, Jeffrey L. Edleson, and Raquel Kennedy Bergen, eds., *Sourcebook on Violence Against Women*. Thousand Oaks, CA: Sage, 2001.

Heise, Lori, Mary Ellsberg, and Megan Gottemoeller. "Ending Violence Against Women." *Population Reports*. Series L, No. 11. Baltimore, MD: Population Information Program, Johns Hopkins University School of Public Health, 1999.

hooks, bell. *Yearning: Race, Gender, and Cultural Politics*. Boston: South End Press, 1990.

Jasinski, Jana L. "Theoretical Explanations for Violence Against Women." In Renzetti et al., eds., *Sourcebook on Violence Against Women*.

Johnson, Ida, and Robert Sigler. "Forced Sexual Intercourse on Campus: Crime or Offensive Behavior?" *Journal of Contemporary Criminal Justice* 12, no. 1, 1996.

Johnson, Michael P. "Patriarchal Terrorism and Common Couple Violence: Two Forms of Violence Against Women in U.S. Families." *Journal of Marriage and the Family* 57, 1995.

Kelly, Liz. *Surviving Sexual Violence*. Cambridge, UK: Polity Press, 1988.

Koss, Mary P., Lisa A. Goodman, Angela Browne, Louise F. Fitzgerald, Gwendolyn Puryear Keita, and Nancy Felipe Russo. *No Safe Haven: Male Violence Against Women at Home, at Work, and in the Community*. Washington, DC: American Psychological Association, 1994.

Koss, Mary P., Lori Heise, and Nancy Felipe Russo. "The Global Health Burden of Rape." In Laura L. O'Toole and Jessica R. Schiffman, eds., *Gender Violence: Interdisciplinary Perspectives*. New York: New York University Press, 1997.

Lopez, Robert. "Firefighters in L.A. Face Bias, U.S. Probe Finds." *Los Angeles Times*, October 3, 2007.

MacKinnon, Catharine. *Sexual Harassment of Working Women: A Case of Sex Discrimination*. New Haven, CT: Yale University Press, 1979.

Mahoney, Patricia, Linda Williams, and Carolyn M. West. "Violence Against Women by Intimate Relationship Partners." In Renzetti et al., eds., *Sourcebook on Violence Against Women*.

Molidor, Christian, and Richard M. Tolman. "Gender and Contextual Factors in Adolescent Dating Violence." *Violence Against Women* 4, no. 2, 1998.

Moore, Crystal Dea, and Caroline K. Waterman. "Predicting Self-Protection Against Sexual Assault in Dating Relationships Among Heterosexual Men and Women, Gay Men, Lesbians and Bisexuals." *Journal of College Student Development* 40, no. 20, 1999.

Office for Victims of Crime. *Strengthening Anti-Stalking Statutes.* Publication no. 189192. Washington, DC: U.S. Department of Justice, 2002.

Price, Lisa. *Feminist Frameworks: Building Theory on Violence Against Women.* Halifax, NS: Fernwood, 2005.

Renzetti, Claire M. *Violent Betrayal: Partner Abuse in Lesbian Relationships.* Thousand Oaks, CA: Sage, 1992.

Richie, Beth E. *Compelled to Crime: The Gender Entrapment of Battered Black Women.* New York: Routledge, 1996.

Richie, Beth E. Plenary Address, Color of Violence: Violence Against Women of Color Conference, Santa Cruz, CA, April, 2000. Cited in Natalie J. Sokoloff, ed., with Christina Pratt. *Domestic Violence at the Margins: Readings on Race, Class, Gender, and Culture.* Piscataway, NJ: Rutgers University Press, 2005.

Rimonte, Nilda. "A Question of Culture: Cultural Approval of Violence Against Women in the Pacific-Asian Community and the Cultural Defense." *Stanford Law Review* 43, no. 6, 1991.

Rozee, Patricia D. "Violence Against Women: Women's Fear of Rape: Causes, Consequences, and Coping." In Joan C. Chrisler, Carla Golden, Patricia D. Rozee, eds., *Lectures on the Psychology of Women.* New York: McGraw-Hill, 2007.

Sellers, Christine, and Max Bromley. "Violent Behavior in College Student Dating Relationships: Implications for Campus Service Providers." *Journal of Contemporary Criminal Justice* 12, no. 1, 1996.

Sheffield, Carole. "Sexual Terrorism." In O'Toole et al., eds., *Gender Violence.*

Stanko, Elizabeth. *Intimate Intrusions: Women's Experience of Male Violence.* London: Routledge and Kegan Paul, 1985. Quoted in Price, *Feminist Frameworks.*

Stark, Evan. *Coercive Control: How Men Entrap Women in Personal Life.* New York: Oxford University Press, 2007.

Straus, Murray A., and Jan E. Stets. "The Marriage License as a Hitting License: A Comparison of Assaults in Dating, Cohabiting, and Married Couples." Paper presented at the Annual Meeting of the American Sociological Association, Atlanta, GA, August 24–28, 1988.

United Nations. *Rome Statute of the International Criminal Court, Part 2: Jurisdiction, Admissibility and Applicable Law (Articles 5–8 defining war crimes).* July 12, 1999.

United Nations General Assembly. *Declaration on the Elimination of Violence Against Women.* Geneva: UN Department of Public Information, 1993.

Wellesley Center for Women Battered Mothers' Testimony Project. *Battered Mothers Speak Out: Human Rights Tribunal on Domestic Violence and Child Custody.* May 9, 2002.

Woo, Elaine. "Eric Monkkonen, 62; UCLA Scholar Studied Murder in N.Y., L.A." *Los Angeles Times,* June 15, 2005.

Wyatt, Gail E., and Monika Reiderle. "The Prevalence and Context of Sexual Harassment Among African American and White American Women." *Journal of Interpersonal Violence* 10, no. 3, 1995.

Yoshioka, Marianne R., and Deborah Y. Choi. "Culture and Interpersonal Violence Research: Paradigm Shift to Create a Full Continuum of Domestic Violence Services." *Journal of Interpersonal Violence* 20, no. 4, 2005.

Yoshioka, Marianne R., Louisa Gilbert, Nabila El-Bassel, and Malahat Baig-Amin. "Social Support and Disclosure of Abuse: Comparing South Asian, African American, and Hispanic Battered Women." *Journal of Family Violence* 18, no. 3, 2003.

Chapter 2

Amnesty International. *Mexico: Ending the Brutal Cycle of Violence Against Women in Ciudad Juárez and the City of Chihuahua.* March 8, 2004.

Amnesty International. *Mexico: Intolerable Killings: Ten Years of Abductions and Murders of Women in Ciudad Juárez and Chihuahua.* August 11, 2003.

Amnesty International. *Pakistan: Honour Killings of Women and Girls.* September 1, 1999.

Ash, Lucy. "India's Dowry Deaths." *BBC News.* July 16, 2003.

Asia Pacific Forum on Women, Law and Development (APWLD), Non-Governmental Organization on the Roster in Consultative Status with the Economic and Social Council of the United Nations (2007), Chiang Mai, Thailand.

Batstone, David. *Not for Sale: The Return of the Global Slave Trade—And How We Can Fight It.* San Francisco: Harper, 2007.

Blumenthal, Max. "Day of the Dead," *Salon,* 2002.

Center for Gender and Refugee Studies, University of California Hastings College of Law. "CGRS Wins En Banc Genital Cutting Case–Abebe." *Newsletter,* Spring 2006.

Chu, Henry. "As India's Wealth Rises, a Woman's Limited Dowry Could Mean Her Death." *Los Angeles Times,* September 22, 2007.

Clarren, Rebecca. "The Invisible Ones." *Ms.,* Summer 2007.

Coalition to Abolish Slavery and Trafficking, *Fact Sheet on Human Trafficking, 2002:* www.castla.org

Coomaraswamy, Radhika. The UN Special Rapporteur on Violence Against Women. Speech on Trafficking in Women, 1995.

Coomaraswamy, Radhika. "Combating Domestic Violence: Obligations of the State." *Innocenti Digest 6.* UNICEF: Innocenti Research Centre, 2000.

Cuomo, Kerry Kennedy. *Speak Truth to Power: Human Rights Defenders Who Are Changing Our World.* Crown Books, 2000. Basis for KLCS-PBS broadcast, "Kennedy Center Presents: Speak Truth to Power," and interview with Rana Husseini, journalist, "Honor Killings in Jordan," October 8, 2000.

Ehrenreich, Nancy, with Mark Barr. "Intersex Surgery, Female Genital Cutting and the Selective Condemnation of 'Cultural Practices.'" *Harvard Civil Rights–Civil Liberties Law Review* 40, no. 1, 2005.

Ertürk, Yakin. *The Due Diligence Standard as a Tool for the Elimination of Violence Against Women.* UN Office of the Special Rapporteur on Violence Against Women, 2006.

Family Violence Prevention Fund. "Laos: The Nation's First Shelter for Women and Children Victimized by Human Trafficking and Domestic Violence Opened in January." *Newsflash*, February 15, 2006.

Garcia-Moreno, Claudia, Lori Heise, Henrica A. F. M. Jansen, Mary Ellsberg, and Charlotte Watts. "Policy Forum: Public Health: Violence Against Women." *Science* 310, 2005.

García-Moreno, Claudia, Henrica A. F. M. Jansen, Mary Ellsberg, Lori Heise, and Charlotte Watts. *WHO Multi-Country Study on Women's Health and Domestic Violence Against Women: Initial Results on Prevalence, Health Outcomes, and Women's Responses.* Geneva: World Health Organization, 2005.

Garrels, Anne. "Concern Grows over Iraqi 'Honor Killings.'" *All Things Considered.* National Public Radio. December 7, 2005.

Gentleman, Amelia. "Indian Brides Pay a High Price." *International Herald Tribune,* November 27, 2006.

Henderson, Sarah, and Alana Jeydel. *Participation and Protest: Women and Politics in a Global World.* New York: Oxford University Press, 2007.

Herbert, Bob. "Punished for Being Female." *International Herald Tribune,* November 3, 2006.

"Honor Killings of Females Soar." *Los Angeles Times.* February 9, 2007.

Immigration Department, Hong Kong Special Administrative Region, in IOM, *Quarterly Bulletin,* April 2001.

James, Stanlie M., and Claire C. Robertson. *Genital Cutting and Transnational Sisterhood: Disputing U.S. Polemics.* Champaign: University of Illinois Press, 2002.

Kang, K. Connie. "Activists Seek Redress for Sex Slaves." *Los Angeles Times,* October 6, 2007.

Krikorian, Greg. "U.S. Grand Jury Indicts Nine in Sex Trafficking Case." *Los Angeles Times,* August 10, 2007.

Kristof, Nicholas D. "Raped, Kidnapped and Silenced." *New York Times,* June 14, 2005.

Kristof, Nicholas D. "The Good Daughter, in a Brothel." *New York Times.* December 17, 2006.

Krug, Etienne G., Linda L. Dahlberg, James A. Mercy, Anthony B. Zwi, and Rafael Lozano, eds. *World Report on Violence and Health.* Geneva: World Health Organization, 2002.

Lavin, Abigail. "Dowry Disgrace: India's 'Kitchen Accident' Epidemic." *Weekly Standard,* November 29, 2006.

Miller, Jody, and Dheeshana Jayasundera. "Prostitution, the Sex Industry, and Sex Tourism." In Renzetti et al., eds., *Sourcebook on Violence Against Women.*

Mittal, Anuradha. "Losing the Farm: How Corporate Globalization Pushes Millions off the Land and into Desperation." (Interview.) *Multinational Monitor* 24, no. 7/8, 2003.

Mohamud, Asha A., Nancy A. Ali, and Nancy V. Yinger. "Executive Summary." *Female Genital Mutilation Programmes to Date: What Works and What Doesn't—A Review.* World Health Organization, 1999.

"Myanmar: Atrocities Against Women Reported." *Los Angeles Times,* February 12, 2007.

"New Ritual to Replace Female Genital Mutilation." *Women's E-News,* May 2003.

Ortiz, Elizabeth Thompson. "Female Genital Mutilation and Public Health: Lessons from the British Experience." *Health Care for Women International* 19, 1998.

Paul, Madan C. *Dowry and Position of Women in India: A Study Of Delhi Metropolis.* New Delhi, India: M. C. Mittal, 1986.

Schneider, Katrin. "Honor Killings in Jordan and Pakistan: Hiding in Prison from Their Own Family." *Qantara.de,* 2005.

Seidband, Debbie. "U.S. Wheat and Corn Exports to Mexico Thrive Under NAFTA (North American Free Trade Agreement)." *AgExporter,* January 2004.

Slackman, Michael. "Voices Rise in Egypt to Shield Girls from an Old Tradition." *New York Times,* September 20, 2007.

"Sudan: Rape Part of Rebel Raid, Aid Group Says." *Los Angeles Times,* January 25, 2007.

United Nations. *Rome Statute of the International Criminal Court, Part 2: Jurisdiction, Admissibility and Applicable Law (Articles 5–8 defining war crimes).* July 12, 1999.

United Nations. *Rome Statute of the International Criminal Court.* December 19, 2003.

United Nations. *Rome Statute of the International Criminal Court: Overview.* December 19, 2003.

United Nations Development Fund for Women (UNIFEM). *World Poverty Day 2007: Investing in Women, Solving the Poverty Puzzle.* Women's Funding Network, 2007.

Wilkinson, Tracy. "Taking the 'Honor' out of Killing Women." *Los Angeles Times,* January 9, 2007.

World Health Organization. *Female Genital Mutilation Programmes: What Works and What Doesn't.* 1999.

World Trade Organization. *What Is the WTO?* July 2007.

Chapter 3

Barnett, Ola W., Cindy Miller-Perrin, and Robin Perrin. *Family Violence Across the Lifespan: An Introduction.* Thousand Oaks, CA: Sage, 2005.

Bergen, ed. *Issues in Intimate Violence.*

Campbell, Jacquelyn, and Karen Soeken. "Women's Responses to Battering over Time: An Analysis of Change." *Journal of Interpersonal Violence* 14, no. 1, 1999.

Catalano, Shannan. *Intimate Partner Violence in the U.S.* U.S. Department of Justice, Bureau of Justice Statistics, 2007.

Dutton, Donald. "Intimate Abusiveness." *Clinical Psychology: Science and Practice* 2, no. 3, 1995.

Dutton, Donald, and Susan Painter. "Traumatic Bonding: The Development of

Emotional Attachments in Battered Women and Other Relationships of Intermittent Abuse." *Victimology: An International Journal* 1, no. 4, 1981.

Graham, Dee L. R., and Edna I. Rawlings. "Bonding with Abusive Dating Partners: Dynamics of Stockholm Syndrome." In Barrie Levy, ed., *Dating Violence: Young Women in Danger.* Berkeley, CA: Seal, 1998.

Gutek, Barbara A., and Mary P. Koss. "Changed Women and Changed Organizations: Consequences of and Coping with Sexual Harassment." *Journal of Vocational Behavior* 42, 1993.

Halpern, Carolyn Tucker, Selene G. Oslak, Mary L. Young, Sandra L. Martin, and Lawrence L. Kupper. "Partner Violence Among Adolescents in Opposite-Sex Romantic Relationships: Findings from the National Longitudinal Study of Adolescent Health." *American Journal of Public Health* 91, no. 10, 2001.

Harris, Maxine, and Roger D. Fallot. *Using Trauma Theory to Design Service Systems.* San Francisco: Jossey-Bass, 2001.

Heise, Lori L., Jacqueline Pitanguy, and Adrienne Germain. *Violence Against Women: The Hidden Health Burden.* World Bank Discussion Paper 255. Washington, DC: World Bank, 1994.

Henderson and Jeydel. *Participation and Protest.*

Herman, Judith. *Trauma and Recovery: The Aftermath of Violence—From Domestic Abuse to Political Terror.* New York: Basic Books, 1992.

Janoff-Bulman, Ronnie. *Shattered Assumptions: Towards a New Psychology of Trauma.* New York: Free Press, 1992.

Koss, Mary P., Lori Heise, and Nancy Felipe Russo. "The Global Health Burden of Rape." In O'Toole et al., eds., *Gender Violence.*

Koss, Mary P., P. G. Koss, and W. J. Woodruff. "Deleterious Effects of Criminal Victimization on Women's Health and Medical Utilization." *Archives of Internal Medicine* 151, no. 2, 1991.

Koss et al. *No Safe Haven.*

Kreisler, Harry. The Case of Trauma and Recovery, Psychological Insight and Political Understanding: Interview with Judith Herman, MD. *University of California Television Presents: Conversations with History.* Berkeley: UCTV, September 21, 2000.

McFarlane, Judith. "Violence During Teen Pregnancy: Health Consequences for Mother and Child." In Levy, ed., *Dating Violence.*

Medea, Andra, and Kathleen Thompson. *Against Rape: A Survival Manual for Women: How to Avoid Entrapment and How to Cope with Rape Physically and Emotionally.* New York: Farrar, Strauss and Giroux, 1974.

Miller, Ted R., Mark A. Cohen, and Brian Wiersema. *Victim Costs and Consequences: A New Look: Research Report.* Washington, DC: U.S. Department of Justice, 1996. Cited in Kathryn E. Moracco, Carol W. Runyan, and Lisa Dulli, *Violence Against Women: Synthesis of Research for Public Health Policy Makers.* National Institute of Justice, 2003.

Moe, Angela M., and Myrtle P. Bell. "The Effects of Battering and Violence on Women's Work and Employability." *Violence Against Women* 10, no. 1, 2004.

Morgan, Phoebe. "Sexual Harassment: Violence Against Women at Work." In Renzetti et al., eds., *Sourcebook on Violence Against Women.*

National Center for Injury Prevention and Control. *Costs of Intimate Partner Violence Against Women in the United States.* Atlanta, GA: Centers for Disease Control and Prevention, 2003.

Novello, Antonia. "From the Surgeon General, U.S. Public Health Service." *Journal of the American Medical Association* 268, no. 11, 1992.

Ortiz. "Female Genital Mutilation and Public Health."

Raymond, Janice G., Jean D'Cunha, Siti Ruhaini Dzuhayatin, H. Patricia Hynes, Zoraida Ramirez Rodriguez, and Aida Santos. *A Comparative Study of Women Trafficked in the Migration Process: Patterns, Profiles and Health Consequences of Sexual Exploitation in Five Countries (Indonesia, the Philippines, Thailand, Venezuela and the United States).* New York: Coalition Against Trafficking in Women, 2002.

Silverman, Jay G., Anita Raj, Lorelei A. Mucci, and Jeanne E. Hathaway. "Dating Violence Against Adolescent Girls and Associated Substance Use, Unhealthy Weight Control, Sexual Risk Behavior, Pregnancy, and Suicidality." *Journal of the American Medical Association* 286, no. 5, 2001.

Stark. *Coercive Control.*

Straus, Murray A., and C. Smith. "Family Patterns of Primary Prevention of Family Violence." In Murray A. Straus and Richard J. Gelles, eds., *Physical Violence in American Families: Risk Factors and Adaptations to Violence in 8,145 Families.* New Brunswick, NJ: Transaction, 1990.

Tjaden, Patricia. "Defining and Measuring Violence Against Women: Background, Issues and Recommendations." Unpublished paper. 2005.

UNICEF Innocenti Research Centre. *Domestic Violence Against Women and Girls,* 2000.

U.S. Department of Health and Human Services. *Healthy People 2000.* Washington, DC: U.S. Department of Health and Human Services: Public Health Services, 1980.

U.S. Department of Health and Human Services. *Surgeon General's Workshop on Violence and Public Health Report.* Washington, DC: U.S. Department of Health and Human Services, Health Resources and Services Administration, 1986.

Chapter 4

Cook, Sarah L., and Mary P. Koss. "More Data Have Accumulated Supporting Date and Acquaintance Rape as Significant Problems for Women." In Donileen R. Loseke, Richard J. Gelles, and Mary M. Cavanaugh, eds., *Current Controversies on Family Violence.* Thousand Oaks, CA: Sage, 2005.

Currie, Dawn H. "Violent Men or Violent Women? Whose Definition Counts?" In Bergen, ed., *Issues in Intimate Violence.*

DeKeseredy, Walter, and Katharine Kelly. "The Incidence and Prevalence of Woman Abuse in Canadian University and College Dating Relationships." *Canadian Journal of Sociology* 18, 1994.

DeKeseredy, Walter, and Linda MacLeod. *Woman Abuse: A Sociological Story.* Toronto: Harcourt Brace, 1997.

DeKeseredy, Walter, and Martin D. Schwartz. "Definitional Issues." In Renzetti et al., eds., *Sourcebook on Violence Against Women.*

Desai, Sujata, and Linda E. Saltzman. "Measurement Issues for Violence Against Women." In Renzetti et al., eds., *Sourcebook on Violence Against Women.*

Faludi, Susan. *Backlash: The Undeclared War Against American Women.* New York: Crown, 1991.

Family Violence Prevention Fund. "Judge Weakens Rape Shield Law in Bryant Case." *NewsFlash,* July 31, 2004.

Frieze, Irene Hanson. "Female Violence Against Intimate Partners: An Introduction." *Psychology of Women Quarterly* 29, 2005.

Gelles, Richard J. "Intimate Violence." In Richard J. Gelles and Murray A. Straus, eds., *Intimate Violence: The Definitive Study of the Causes and Consequences of Abuse in the American Family.* New York: Simon & Schuster, 1988.

Giggans, Patti. Personal communication. December 15, 2007.

Gilbert, Neil. "Advocacy Research Overstates the Incidence of Date and Acquaintance Rape." In Loseke et al., eds., *Current Controversies on Family Violence.*

Golden, Kristen. "The Not So Fine Print." *Ms.,* Sept./Oct. 1994.

Gornick, Janet, Martha R. Burt, and Karen J. Pittman. "Structure and Activities of Rape Crisis Centers in the Early 1980s." *Crime & Delinquency* 31, no. 2, 1985.

Graves, Kelly N., Stacy M. Sechrist, Jacquelyn W. White, and Matthew J. Paradise. "Intimate Partner Violence Perpetrated by College Women Within the Context of a History of Victimization." *Psychology of Women Quarterly* 29, 2005.

Hammer, Rhonda. *Antifeminism and Family Terrorism: A Critical Feminist Perspective.* Lanham, MD: Rowman and Littlefield, 2002.

hooks. *Yearning.*

Jones, Ann. *Next Time She'll Be Dead: Battering and How to Stop It.* Boston: Beacon Press, 1994.

Jones, Ann. *Women Who Kill.* Boston: Beacon Press, 1996.

Koss, Mary P., Christine A. Gidycz, and Nadine Wisniewski. "The Scope of Rape: Incidence and Prevalence of Sexual Aggression and Victimization in a National Sample of Higher Education Students." *Journal of Consulting and Clinical Psychology* 55, no. 2, 1987.

Koss et al. *No Safe Haven.*

Kuehl, Sheila. "Seeing Is Believing: Research on Women's Sexual Orientation and Public Policy." *Journal of Social Issues* 56, no. 2, 2000.

LaViolette, Alyce. Personal communication, 2007.

Lithwick, Dahlia. "Gag Order: A Nebraska Judge Bans Word 'Rape' from his Courtroom." *Slate,* June 20, 2007.

Loseke, Donileen R., and Demie Kurz. "Men's Violence Toward Women Is the Serious Social Problem." In Loseke et al., eds., *Current Controversies on Family Violence.*

McHugh, Maureen C., Nichole A. Livingston, and Amy Ford. "A Postmodern Approach to Women's Use of Violence: Developing Multiple and Complex Conceptualizations." *Psychology of Women Quarterly* 29, 2005.

Merriam-Webster's Collegiate Dictionary, 11th ed. Springfield, MA: Merriam-Webster, 2006.

Mills, Linda. 2002 speech (untitled), quoted in Deborah Sontag. "Fierce Entanglements." *New York Times Magazine,* November 17, 2002.

Mills, Linda G. "Killing Her Softly: Intimate Abuse and the Violence of State Intervention." *Harvard Law Review* 113, 1999.

Price. *Feminist Frameworks.*

Richie, Beth E. "A Black Feminist Reflection on the Antiviolence Movement." In Sokoloff, ed., *Domestic Violence at the Margins.*

Schechter, Susan. *Women and Male Violence: The Visions and Struggles of the Battered Women's Movement.* Boston: South End Press, 1982.

Sokoloff, Natalie. "Introduction: Frameworks and Overarching Themes." In Sokoloff, ed., *Domestic Violence at the Margins.*

Sokoloff, Natalie, and Ida Dupont. "Domestic Violence: Examining the Intersection of Race, Class, and Gender." In Sokoloff, ed., *Domestic Violence at the Margins.*

Stark. *Coercive Control.*

Stern, Seth. "Bryant Case Tests Limits of 'Rape Shield Laws.'" *Christian Science Monitor,* October 22, 2003.

Straus, Murray A. "Women's Violence Toward Men Is a Serious Social Problem." In Loseke et al., eds., *Current Controversies on Family Violence.*

Straus, Murray A., Sherry L. Hamby, Sue Boney-McCoy, and David B. Sugarman. "The Revised Conflict Tactics Scale (CTS2): Development and Preliminary and Psychometric Data." *Journal of Family Issues* 17, no. 3, 1996.

Websdale, Neil. "Nashville: Domestic Violence and Incarcerated Women in Poor Black Neighborhoods." In Sokoloff, ed., *Domestic Violence at the Margins.*

Wyatt, Dr. Gail Elizabeth. *Stolen Women: Reclaiming Our Sexuality, Taking Back Our Lives.* New York: Wiley and Sons, 1997.

Zwerling, Elizabeth. "Suit Presses for 'Gender Symmetry' in Shelters." *Women's E-News,* July 21, 2003.

Chapter 5

Access Denied: U.S. Restrictions on International Family Planning: www.Globalgagrule.org

Amnesty International. *About the Stop Violence Against Women Campaign:* www .amnestyusa.org/stopviolence

Barry, Kathleen. *Female Sexual Slavery.* New York: Avon, 1979.

Bertone, Andrea. "Transnational Activism to Combat Trafficking in Persons." *Brown Journal of World Affairs* 10, no. 2, 2004.

Boateng, Michael. "Girls of Banda." *Ghanaian Chronicle* newspaper, December 11, 2006, as it appeared in the August 2007 newsletter of the Inter-African Committee on Traditional Practices Affecting the Health of Women and Children (IAC).

Brownmiller, Susan. *In Our Time: Memoir of a Revolution.* New York: Dell, 1999.

Buncab, Imelda. Training director, Coalition to Abolish Slavery and Trafficking. Personal conversation. November 29, 2007.

Buzawa, Eve S., and Carl G. Buzawa. *Domestic Violence: The Criminal Justice Response.* Thousand Oaks, CA: Sage, 2002.

Ciezaldo, Annia. "For Iraqi Women, Abu Ghraib's Taint." *The Christian Science Monitor,* May 28, 2004.

Clothesline Project: www.clotheslineproject.org

Coalition for Sexual and Bodily Rights in Muslim Societies: www.wwhr.org/csbr.php

Coalition to Abolish Slavery and Trafficking: www.castla.org

Coleman, Isobel. "Women, Islam, and the New Iraq." *Foreign Affairs,* Jan./Feb. 2006.

Dorkenoo, Efua. Testimony Before the Equal Opportunities Committee, Scottish Parliament, December 14, 2004. In Scottish Parliament, "Equal Opportunities Committee Official Report 14 December 2004: Prohibition of Female Genital Mutilation Bill," 2004.

Dworkin, Andrea. "Pornography and Grief," in Laura Lederer, ed., *Take Back the Night: Women on Pornography.* New York: William Morrow, 1980.

EPCAT International: www.ecpat.net

Ferree, Myra Marx, and Mangala Subramaniam. "Activism," in Cheris Kramarae, Dale Spender, eds., *Routledge International Encyclopedia of Women: Global Women's Issues and Knowledge, Volume 1: Ability to Education.* New York: Routledge, 2000.

Giggans. Personal communication.

Gruber Foundation. "Turkish Activist and Two Organizations She Leads to Share $500K 2007 Gruber Foundation International Women's Rights Prize." Press release, July 18, 2007.

Hart, Barbara J. (1999). *Opening Celebration.* Next Millennium Conference: Ending Domestic Violence, August 29, 1999. Published September 2000 by the U.S. Department of Justice, document number 184562.

Henderson et al. *Participation and Protest.*

Horowitz, Carl F. "Female Genital Mutilation: Understanding and Overcoming a Worldwide Sexual Crime." *Women's Freedom Network Working Paper,* Summer 2002.

Inter-African Committee on Traditional Practices Affecting the Health of Women and Children (IAC): www.iac-ciaf.com/publications

Jackman, Jennifer, and Christine Onyango. *Reports from Beijing.* Feminist Majority Foundation, 1995.

Joseph, Suad, ed. *Encyclopedia of Women and Islamic Cultures, Vol. 3.* Boston: Brill Leiden, 2005.

Kahn, Nida. "WMC Exclusive: Muslim Women, Taking the Lead." *Women's Media Center,* November 8, 2007.

Katz, Jackson. *The Macho Paradox: Why Some Men Hurt Women and How All Men Can Help.* Naperville, IL: Sourcebooks, 2006.

Ko, Carolyn N. *Civil Restraining Orders for Domestic Violence: The Unresolved Question of "Efficacy."* Monograph, University of Southern California Law School, 2002.

Koss et al. *No Safe Haven.*

Marx, Jeffrey. "He Turns Boys into Men." *Parade,* Aug. 29, 2004.

Ministry of Foreign Affairs of the People's Republic of China. "The Fourth World Conference on Women Met in Beijing in September, 1995." From www.chinaembassy canada.org

Pence, Ellen. "Advocacy on Behalf of Battered Women." In Renzetti et al., eds., *Sourcebook on Violence Against Women.*

Rape, Abuse and Incest National Network (RAINN): www.rainn.org

Raphael, Jody, and Richard M. Tolman. *Trapped by Poverty, Trapped by Abuse: New Evidence Documenting the Relationship Between Domestic Violence and Welfare.* Chicago: Taylor Institute, 1997.

Rosenbluth, Helene. Personal conversation. November 25, 2007.

Schechter. *Women and Male Violence.*

Sherman, Lawrence W., and Richard A. Berk. "The Specific Deterrent Effects of Arrest for Domestic Violence." *American Sociological Review* 49, no. 2, 1984.

Slaughter, Ruth. Personal interview. December 14, 2007.

Smith, Andrea. "Looking to the Future: Domestic Violence, Women of Color, the State, and Social Change." In Sokoloff, ed., *Domestic Violence at the Margins.*

Soler, Esta. "The Next Frontier: Engaging More Men in Efforts to Stop Domestic Violence." *News from the Homefront,* Family Violence Prevention Fund, Fall/Winter 2000.

United Nations. *Rome Statute of the International Criminal Court.* December 19, 2003: www.un.org/law/icc

United Nations Division for the Advancement of Women, Department of Economic and Social Affairs. "Fourth World Conference on Women, Beijing, China," 1995.

Yamaguchi, Nori. Director, Aware, Tokyo. Personal communication. July 14, 2007.

INDEX

ACKNOWLEDGMENTS

This book reflects many sources of my education about violence. For thirty-seven years, my most influential teachers have been survivors: women, girls, and communities who have recovered from violence, become stronger, and contributed to the changes that benefit all of us today.

My students at UCLA have taught me a great deal from their questions, thoughts, and stories, and the ways in which they have sorted out personal experiences with violence through their studies.

I owe a great deal to professor Chris Littleton, chair of the women's studies department, Mary Margaret Smith, Samantha Hogan, and others in the department for many years of encouragement and support. Nora Zepeda was very helpful to me in gathering books and articles in the earliest stages of writing this book.

I am lucky to have had so many inspiring women with tireless energy—movers and shakers for social change—among my colleagues and close friends all of these years. We have intense discussions and debates, challenge and learn from one another, cheer each other on, laugh together, and share frustrations and successes. While writing about the history of these movements for fundamental change in thinking about women and violence, I am reminded that this work takes many people, all doing their parts. This keeps me from being overwhelmed by how much more there is to do.

I am grateful to Patti Giggans, my longtime friend and coconspirator in the long march to prevent violence against women, for her wonderful ideas and her feedback.

I am especially indebted to Anne Mathews, my editor, who suffered through long hours along with me, emailing one another as we worked. Anne has a brilliant command of the language and the subject. She is remarkably clear in conceptualizing and articulating ideas—succinctly and "spot on." She was always gentle, considerate, and patient, even when having to give me bad news. I appreciate Seal Press, a publisher dedicated to improving women's lives, for our long and fruitful relationship. Faith Conlon, Ingrid Emerick, Denise Silva, Anne Mathews, and others have made producing my books enjoyable and satisfying.

Linda, my partner, adviser, supporter, and cheerleader—I couldn't do any of this without her.

The motivation for this book and my work is the future: my grandchildren and girls in every corner of the world and their freedom from fear.

ABOUT THE AUTHOR

Barrie Levy is a licensed clinical social worker in private practice and a faculty member in the Department of Social Welfare, School of Public Policy, and the Women's Studies Department at the University of California, Los Angeles. She is the editor of *Dating Violence: Young Women in Danger,* an anthology on teen dating violence, and the author of *In Love and in Danger: A Teen's Guide to Breaking Free of Abusive Relationships;* she cowrote (with Patricia Giggans) the books *What Parents Need to Know About Dating Violence: Advice and Support for Helping Your Teen* and *Fifty Ways to a Safer World: Everyday Actions You Can Take to Prevent Violence in Neighborhoods, Schools and Communities.* During thirty years as an activist to stop violence against women, she has founded and directed four domestic and sexual violence organizations. She is a nationally recognized speaker and trainer and has appeared on more than fifteen television shows.

© LINDA GARNETS

CREDITS

Chapter 1

"Women practicing self-defense" photo was provided by Barrie Levy.

Excerpts and adapted material from Liz Kelly's *Surviving Sexual Violence* reprinted by permission of Polity Press.

Excerpted material from Carole Sheffield's "Sexual Terrorism" is reprinted with permission of the author.

Surviving Sexual Violence reprinted by permission of Polity Press.

Excerpts from *Coercive Control: How Men Entrap Women in Personal Life* © 2007 Evan Stark. Reprinted by permission of Oxford University Press.

Excerpts from Shamita Das Dasgupta's "Women's Realities: Defining Violence Against Women by Immigration, Race, and Class" reprinted courtesy of Sage Publications. Originally published in Raquel Kennedy Bergen, ed., *Issues in Intimate Violence*.

Excerpts from Sarah Deer's "Ask Amnesty" is reprinted courtesy of Amnesty International USA (www.amnestyusa.org).

Excerpted material from bell hooks's *Yearning: Race, Gender, and Cultural Politics* is reprinted courtesy of South End Press.

Chapter 2

"Marcha contra el femicidio" photo is reprinted by permission of the photographer, Fernanda Trivelli.

Max Blumenthal's "Day of the Dead" originally published by Salon.com. Excerpt reprinted courtesy of the publisher.

Chapter 3

Collage image on page 72 is reprintd by permission of the artist, Ginny Fleming.

Excerpts from *Coercive Control: How Men Entrap Women in Personal Life* © 2007 Evan Stark. Reprinted by permission of Oxford University Press.

Chapter 4

Poster from the Family Violence Prevention Fund is reprinted by permission of www .endabuse.org.

Excerpts from *Next Time She'll Be Dead* by Ann Jones (c) 1994 by Ann Jones. Reprinted by permission of Beacon Press, Boston.

Excerpts from *Coercive Control: How Men Entrap Women in Personal Life* (c) 2007 Evan Stark. Reprinted by permission of Oxford University Press, Inc.

Excerpts from Maureen McHugh, Nichole Livingston, and Amy Ford's "A Postmodern Approach to Women's Use of Violence: Developing Multiple and Complex Conceptualizations" originally appeared in *Psychology of Women Quarterly.* Reprinted courtesy of Wiley-Blackwell Publishing.

Excerpts from Rhonda Hammer's *Antifeminism and Family Terrorism: A Critical Feminist Perspective* reprinted courtesy of Rowman and Littlefield Publishing Group.

Chapter 5

The Clothesline Project photograph was provided by and is reprinted with permission of The Associated Press.

Excerpts from Barbara J. Hart's August 29, 1999, speech at the Next Millennium Conference reprinted courtesy of Barbara J. Hart.

Excerpt from Jackson Katz's *The Macho Paradox: Why Some Men Hurt Women and How All Men Can Help* reprinted courtesy of Sourcebooks.

SELECTED TITLES FROM SEAL PRESS

For more than thirty years, Seal Press has published groundbreaking books. By women. For women. Visit our website at www.sealpress.com and our blog at www.sealpress.com/blog.

Transgender History by Susan Stryker. $12.95, 1-58005-224-X. An introduction to transgender history from the mid–19th century through today.

Listen Up: Voices from the Next Feminist Generation edited by Barbara Findlen. $16.95, 1-58005-054-9. A collection of essays featuring the voices of today's young feminists on racism, sexuality, identity, AIDS, revolution, abortion, and much more.

Colonize This: Young Women of Color on Today's Feminism edited by Daisy Hernández and Bushra Rehman. $16.95, 1-58005-067-0. An insight into a new generation of brilliant, outspoken women of color, how they are speaking to the concerns of a new feminism, and their place in it.

Intimate Politics: How I Grew Up Red, Fought for Free Speech, and Became a Feminist Rebel by Bettina F. Aptheker. $16.95, 1-58005-160-X. A courageous and uncompromising account of one woman's personal and political transformation, and a fascinating portrayal of a key chapter in our nation's history.

The Maternal Is Political: Women Writers at the Intersection of Motherhood and Social Change edited by Shari MacDonald Strong. $15.95, 1-58005-243-6. Exploring the vital connection between motherhood and social change, *The Maternal Is Political* features thirty powerful literary essays by women striving to make the world a better place for children and families—both their own and other women's.

Invisible Girls: The Truth about Sexual Abuse by Dr. Patti Feuereisen with Caroline Pincus. $15.95, 1-58005-135-9. An important book for teenage girls, young women, and those who care about them, that gives hope and encouragement to sexual abuse survivors by letting them know that they're not alone and that there are many roads to healing.